FOR A GREATER PURPOSE

To Joanie —
All Glory be to God!
Zip Rzeppa

ZIP RZEPPA
MY LIFE JOURNEY

MATER
MEDIA

Published by Mater Media
St. Louis, Missouri
www.matermedia.org

Cover and Interior Design: Trese Gloriod
Back cover photo: www.flickr.com / people / jlhopgood /
Editor: Cathy Gilmore

Printed in the USA.

978-0-9913542-1-4

In gratitude to my mom, Millie,
for giving me life, faith,
and a love for storytelling

A beautiful child of God. I had no idea what lay ahead.

INTRODUCTION

Welcome to my world. A world in which an ordinary, middle class kid from Detroit with no major contacts or impressive wealth or genius can wind up in some pretty amazing places.

Like going to school with Howard Stern. Lounging poolside with Johnny Bench during spring training. Negotiating with Kareem Abdul-Jabbar in the living room of his California home. Hanging with the greatest female athlete of the 20th century. Creating national radio shows for Dick Vitale and Dan Dierdorf. Helping Joe Buck get his start in TV. Traveling the world with Bill O'Reilly.

Then God *rocked* my world when He teamed me up with a different set of superstars.

Like the woman with multiple disabilities whose life touched thousands. The challenged man who sang the national anthem in front of 47,000 people. The suffering, out-of-work laborer who helped repair the homes of a thousand senior citizens. The once-homeless man whose video raked in big bucks for the poor.

In my desire to *share* my world, I dated dazzling TV reporters, brilliant doctors, an intriguing counselor, a fascinating linguist, a gymnastics star, and many others before I finally found the *perfect* woman. She may surprise you!

You see, my world is full of the spiritual serendipity of seemingly chance encounters in the hands of a loving God.

A God who definitely has a sense of humor!

HEART IN HAND

I was desperate to get a date.

After serving a four-year sentence at an all-boys high school in Detroit, I was roaming free in the vibrant city of Boston. Ah, Boston University. College girls everywhere! I was looking for Barbie, but unfortunately, I didn't look like Ken. Picture a young George Costanza.

After weeks with no love connection, I had to take action! I figured plenty of young beauties would enjoy a concert by the red-hot band, Creedence Clearwater Revival, and it just so happened they were coming into town.

In utter brilliance, I whipped up a contest. *Win a Free Ticket to see CCR!* Of course, the lucky winner would be escorted by *me!* I placed colorful flyers with pull-tabs listing my dorm room phone in the cafeterias and—zeroing in even more—in the girls' dorms.

What genius! How many girls would respond? If there were too many, I'd slap a limit on it. In any case, we'd get to the next step—

3

personal interviews! I knew it might be tough to sort through the finalists, but hey, I could handle it.

My friends were appalled. They thought I was nuts. *What the hell are you doing?* My roommate was petrified someone would recognize our shared phone number, and mock *him* for *my* insanity.

For some reason, the shared phone wasn't ringing. I figured I must have mis-typed the number. Horrified, I wondered what lucky guy was getting all my calls! After a few days, I had to face the truth—not a single contestant came forward. I couldn't believe it.

Undaunted, I jumped on the subway and headed to Boston Garden. Alone. As usual. But I was filled with renewed hope. I was clutching an extra ticket, and the concert was a sellout!

Surely some babes would be hanging outside, forlorn that they couldn't get in. I would be their hero. I puffed up my chest, and began to look around.

There she was! A cute little blonde, nice figure, attractive, but not a knockout. That was good. Not out of my league! Who knew what our future might hold?

I coyly waved the extra ticket as I approached. She almost fainted. "Oh, thank you! *THANK YOU,*" she squealed. I thought about holding hands, but I didn't want to rush things.

Between "Travelin' Band" and "Who'll Stop the Rain," I discovered "Suzie-Q" was an art major at Emerson College. I could learn to appreciate art! As we sang and cheered and jumped and danced to the tunes, I was racking my brains to come up with a suave way to ask for her phone number.

The moment CCR finished its explosive encore, I looked into her eyes. Before I could speak, she said, "Thank you *so much!* That was *great!*"

And she vanished.

Apparently, she didn't want any Zip in her life.

The crowd pushed past me. As my shoes stuck to the beer-saturated floor of the Garden, I tried to make sense of it. *What just happened? Was that a date? We shared the concert for sure, but—we didn't go out to eat. Not even coffee.* I knew I'd never see her again. Did it count?

No matter, I was just getting started.

I knew there was *someone* out there who would appreciate my creativity and passion. Life was exciting, and I was determined to find the perfect woman with whom to share the adventure.

STARTING OUT

A HANDFUL OF JOY

The Perfect Woman would be a reflection of someone I already knew. The ideal was Imelda Mary McIntyre "Millie" Rzeppa. My mom. She radiated joy.

To say Mom was full of life is like saying the ocean is full of water.

In my childhood, Mom was the center of a wheel with spokes of familiar faith-filled symmetry. In our Detroit cul-de-sac in the 1950s, we were all Catholic. All the moms and dads were married, and only to each other. Everyone's kids played at everyone's houses. My young life had the charm and character of a Norman Rockwell print fueled with the energy of my indefatigable mom.

But she was no iconic June Cleaver. She was smarter. And far funnier. She earned a master's degree in the 1940s, a time when many women didn't attend college. A spunky Irish storytelling school teacher, she left the classroom to enrich the education of me and my two younger brothers, and later went on to become an extremely successful residential realtor. In every role, she showered those around her with wit, wisdom, and love.

She inspired me—and countless others—with her supremely optimistic outlook, cheerful demeanor and the belief that everything's going to be okay no matter what. Her love and compassion for all people flowed from a genuine deep faith in God and an all-out love for everyone in Heaven, from the Trinity to the Blessed Mother to the saints and the angels.

I could tell you a million Mom stories, but I'll limit it to one. Fast forward to a trip we took to Ireland. Mom was 72. I was 40, and old enough to fully appreciate what a one-of-a-kind jewel she was. The trip was a capstone of a great relationship. We were with a tour group of 30 people from America. Everyone was sharing stories about their ancestors.

My mom said, "Three of my grandparents were born in Ireland, and one was born in Scotland." Pausing for effect, she added, "So I'm Irish with a shot of Scotch!"

Not all of our traveling companions shared Mom's joy of life. In particular, two New Yorkers. Brothers. One was a retired police officer, and the other an insurance salesman. I sensed trouble.

Absolutely loving every minute of the tour, Mom said to one of the Bowery Boys, "Isn't this great?" With a bored look, he responded, "I'd rather be on a beach, sipping a cocktail." Mom's mouth dropped open. I thought she was going to slap him.

We visited the House of Waterford Crystal where the finest crystal on the planet is cut by artisans who spend ten years as apprentices before they are trusted to cut the masterpieces for the market. Many of us bought treasures, as they were priced far below the imported prices in the States.

Mom was beside herself when the New Yorkers purchased large wooden wall clocks. "Who on earth buys a *wooden clock* at the Waterford *Crystal* Factory!"

When we got to Blarney Castle, we discovered 125 rough, ancient concrete steps leading to the top where the Blarney Stone is imbedded. When you get up there, you have to get down on your back, extend from the waist out over the side of the castle, and then reach your lips up, in order to make the kiss.

Mom had a mild heart condition, so I said, "You know, Mom, you don't have to climb all the way up there. I can go up and kiss it for you."

She glared at me in disbelief. "I didn't come all the way to Ireland to *not* kiss the Blarney Stone."

Then she looked at one of the New Yorkers, the former cop, and said, "Are you going up?"

He got this pained look on his face and said, "No, I don't think so. I've got a little problem with my back, and—"

My mom cut him off. The former teacher smiled and took him to school. "Wimp! Let me show you how it's done."

Mom, *of course,* made it all the way up and kissed the Stone, and made sure she got pictures to prove it. Mom kissed all of life with the same determination, and I loved her for it.

HOLDING HIS HAND

Two years after our trip, my dad was diagnosed with Alzheimer's disease. In her typical, personal, caring way, Mom refused to put him in a care facility. Instead, with the help of one of my brothers and part-time nurses, she stayed by his side during the long goodbye.

Dad could recall raising the family, but he had no recollection of how he had made a living, working as a car salesman for decades in the Motor City. My mom showed him the nine rings he won as the top selling Cadillac salesman in Michigan, but he responded with a kindly gaze as if she was talking about someone else.

This quiet, caring family man was the perfect stoic German counterpart to my vivacious Irish mother. Dad was an exemplary faithful husband and loving father whose advice when I was young, stayed with me all of my life—"Whatever you do, do it to the best of your ability." Dad spoke more with his solid, principled actions than with words, and I treasure every memory of him.

In the final year of his life, when he could not talk and had lost most of his faculties, he *spoke* to my Mom through a boyish smile he beamed as she brought him his nightly ice cream. The loving rapport between Mom and Dad, even at the end, was an honor to witness and a model I longed to follow in my life.

GETTING A GRIP

I was the oldest of three boys, and if Mom hadn't suffered the miscarriage of three *more boys,* we would have had our own hockey team. There were no girls, which partially explains why I grew up thinking that females were exotic, foreign creatures.

When I was five, my mom's aging parents moved in with us.

My grandfather was a tall, rugged, native Easterner who had made a pretty good living as an engineer. He often displayed a rather gruff personality, but he was a softie around me. As a big baseball fan, he would regale me with stories about the exploits of Babe Ruth and Ty Cobb. Some of the tales were repetitious, but I never got tired of hearing them. There's a certain romance to a gray-haired old man imparting baseball history to a beloved grandchild.

Two memories about my Granny stick in my mind. First, she could not walk without the aid of crutches, and second, she loved to sit with me and watch professional *wrestling*. Actually, Granny did more than just watch. She *participated*. She'd swing a crutch at the old black-and-white screen and scream as Killer Kowalski mercilessly applied his dreaded "Claw Hold" to the midsection of his unfortunate opponent. For all the world, it looked like Granny was suffering right along with the poor guy on the mat.

We especially loved Haystacks Calhoun, who at 600 pounds certainly approximated the size of a haystack. He'd enter the ring in overalls because they didn't make tights big enough to fit him. He'd swing his Lucky Horse Shoe around on a chain, then hang it on the ring post. His greatest "skill" was "The Big Splash" in which he'd get his opponent down, and then simply jump on top of him. The "Splash" brought many victories to ol' Haystacks, and the closing bell would always bring us to our feet, Granny pumping both crutches toward the ceiling, and me, punching the air in delight. The WWE was decades away, but pro wrestling had a firm grip on Granny and me.

A TOUCH OF HUMOR

I survived eight years of Catholic grade school. Humor was my lifeline. In fourth grade, my teacher came to understand that I was full of laughs, so she'd let me get up during art class and tell jokes while the other kids finished their projects. I began to think I had serious potential as a stand-up comedian. Before long, I was sitting in the back of the classroom, snapping jokes non-stop.

Well, when the semester ended, my report card reflected all A's—with the exception of a D in conduct and courtesy. Naturally, my parents demanded an explanation. Somehow they didn't go for my "Hey, the jokes were really funny!" response.

My ill-timed comedy routines merited me three or four lashes from my dad's belt. *Miraculously,* I grew up to be a well-adjusted adult without intervention from Child Protective Services. I did my best to reel in the comedy act, and managed to get a B in conduct and courtesy the next semester. Dad was disappointed it wasn't an A, but he spared me corporal punishment.

Rub-A-Dub-Dub, Saving Water in the Tub
With my two younger brothers, Gerry on the left, and Joe on the right

HANDING IT DOWN

I further developed my intellect, wit, and passion for sports at Brother Rice High School in suburban Detroit. I was among the herd of 1,000 boys shepherded by the Christian Brothers of Ireland. These men in black were strict but spirited, with their youthful zeal and enthusiasm setting the tone. One day we showed up for school and found the Brothers had painted our football team's bus in one of our school colors---*neon orange*. Whenever we traveled to road games, there was no mistaking when Brother Rice had arrived.

The good Brothers demanded respect for more than just our school colors when Steve Jones came to school. He was the first black student to walk the halls of Brother Rice. He and I were freshmen in 1966, and we quickly became best friends. Steve came to our home many times— making him the first black person other than a laborer to visit our white suburban neighborhood. My parents treated him like their own son.

We shared a passion for sports. In fact, Steve was there after football practice the day I got the nickname that would stay with me for life. The sports editor of the school newspaper saw me throwing the ball around with a lot of "zip" and said, "Hey, Christopher, they should call you 'Zip' Rzeppa!" In *every subsequent edition* of the school newspaper, that became my name, and in our sports-crazed, all-boys school, the name stuck.

The Brothers who coached us were tough. Brother Duffy was the football team's defensive coordinator. During an early-season game in stifling heat, we gathered on our neon bus at halftime to mount a come-back strategy. Our hefty defensive tackle, John Fontanesi, fell asleep. All eyes were on Brother Duffy as he deftly strolled down the aisle and brought Big John to consciousness with a smack to the face. Fontanesi went on to play college football, which probably didn't seem too chal-lenging after his four years of tough love from Brother Duffy.

Avoiding confrontations with the good Brother, Steve and I went to war together on the gridiron for four years. Steve played running back and wide receiver, and was one of the most talented players in the state. To understate, I did not quite measure up. I broke my leg my sophomore year, started only one game as a junior, and then was benched by a new coach in favor of an underclassman as a senior. But when I got to start at quarterback in the last game of the year, I was more than ready.

The game was against the neighboring public school, Seaholm High. The public vs. Catholic rivalry was fierce. Steve scored the only touchdown of the first quarter on a 55-yard run. Then we opened things up. I fired three touchdown passes in the second quarter, the longest of which went to Steve, and at halftime, good ol' Brother Rice had an incredible 32-0 lead. The coach played the underclassmen in the second half as Steve and I strutted on the sidelines drinking Cokes, basking in the glory of our triumphant final game.

The last game of our high school basketball careers had a much different ending. We faced Pontiac Central in the District Finals of the State Tournament. Pontiac Central was an all-black public school located eight miles from Brother Rice. It was very close to Steve Jones' home. Rather than attend Pontiac Central, Steve had made the courageous choice to become the first black student at Brother Rice in search of a high quality Catholic education.

We had a good team, but we were clearly overmatched. After all, Pontiac Central had Campanella "Campy" Russell, the future All-American at the University of Michigan who played nine years in the NBA. A couple of Campy's teammates were almost as good.

Steve was our best player and he fought his heart out, but by the fourth quarter, Pontiac Central was putting the game away. It was at this point that the all-black Pontiac Central crowd began with the verbal abuse. It started with cries of "Uncle Tom!" and grew worse from there.

It was sickening to hear parents and adults cursing at Steve and yelling "Deserter!" and "Fool!" When Steve, obviously rattled, put up an air ball, the Pontiac Central crowd roared in derision. They were merciless.

Afterwards, in the locker room, Steve and I hugged each other and cried our eyes out. Only Steve could know what it was like to take the fans' abuse. I tried to console him but I knew that words would be inadequate. At the same time, we shared another sadness. After four years at Brother Rice, this would be the last game we ever played together. I tried to whisper to Steve about all the victories we shared, but at this moment, it seemed hollow.

It was only later that I realized that life is bigger than sports. If Steve had gone to Pontiac Central, he would have been on the team that went on to win the State Championship. But he and I never would have met—and never would have shared a deep, warm, uncondi-tional friendship.

My friend, Hazim Abdullahrauf, whose name was Steve Jones
when he broke the color barrier at Brother Rice High

HAND OVER FIST

All of us at Brother Rice rooted for the Detroit Tigers, who during my high school years, ended up playing one of the most significant sociological roles in American sports history.

In 1964, the Civil Rights Act was passed to assure that blacks would have freedom and equality under the law. Well, freedom and equality weren't coming fast enough, and in the summer of 1967, Detroit was torn apart by race riots. Scores of angry and impoverished blacks set stores on fire, smashed windows, and looted businesses. Chaos reigned on the streets. Law enforcement personnel attempted to restore order, sometimes blasting the rioters with fire hoses. Gunfights ensued. 43 people died. A curfew was enacted that lasted for the duration of the summer.

When Dr. Martin Luther King Jr. was murdered in Memphis the next April, there was widespread apprehension that Detroit would be in for another long, hot, violent summer. That's when the Detroit Tigers—unexpectedly, inadvertently, and unintentionally—stepped up to the proverbial plate.

The 1968 Tigers were led by my all-time favorite baseball player, Al Kaline. The future Hall of Famer was in his 16th major league season, but he had only seen the World Series on TV. I think it was a bigger deal to me than it was to Kaline that he get to play in the Series. Al's chances were helped by a young pitcher who not so many years later would be sentenced to prison for more than 20 years as a convicted felon. His name was Denny McLain, and that season he won 31 games, more than anyone in 34 years, and more than anyone has won in a season since.

Kaline and McLain were white. They were team leaders, along with two super popular black players, Willie Horton and Gates

Brown. Horton was a young, power hitting outfielder who came out of Detroit's inner city Public High School League. Brown came out of a penitentiary. He was given the nickname 'Gates' because in penal recreation games, he kept hitting the ball over the prison gates. In 1968, he was perhaps the best pinch-hitter in the American League.

That summer, Detroiters both black and white, banded together and cheered on the Tigers as they tore apart the American League and advanced to their first World Series since 1945.

But the fun didn't end there. Facing the defending World Champion St. Louis Cardinals, the underdog Tigers rallied from a 3-1 deficit in games—thanks in part to a clutch 8th inning game-tying single by Al Kaline in Game 5—to even the Fall Classic at three games apiece.

But the Tigers were a huge underdog in the deciding Game 7. They were on the road, going against baseball's most dominant pitcher, Bob Gibson, who had whiffed 17 Tigers in Game 1, a World Series strikeout record that has never been matched. Yes, the same Bob Gibson who was the winning pitcher in Game 7 of the World Series in 1964, and again in the previous Series in '67.

The Tigers countered with a pitcher known as "The Fat Man." Mickey Lolich routinely brought his oversized girth to the ballpark on a motorcycle. After he retired, he spent his days as the proprietor of a donut shop. But in '68, Lolich was the winning pitcher in World Series Games 2 and 5, so we had hope. But not much. The Fat Man had to pitch on only two days of rest.

Well, Game 7 was scoreless until the sixth inning as Gibson and Lolich matched each other in excellence. In the top of the 6th inning, with two on and two out, the Tigers' Jim Northrup hit a screaming line drive into centerfield. Curt Flood misjudged the ball, and it sailed over his head for a two-run triple. The next batter singled, and the Tigers had a 3-0 lead.

The Fat Man pitched a complete game as the Tigers won Game 7, 4-1, to become the World Champs.

That night, thousands of black *and* white Detroiters headed to the airport to greet their heroes as the team charter returned from St. Louis. What happened was unprecedented. Tens of thousands of people *swarmed out onto the runway* at Detroit Metropolitan Airport, making it impossible for the plane to land.

They had to divert the flight to an auxiliary airport nearby. And even though the tens of thousands of fans at Detroit Metro did not get to greet their heroes in person, there were no riots, no fights, and no disorder. Detroit came together to celebrate its World Championship, and nothing was going to disturb the peace. Or the joy.

At the age of 16, I had witnessed the power of sports to bring people together.

REACHING OUT

The only person at Brother Rice who wasn't thrilled at the Tigers title was the young, baby-faced Brother Ross Weilatz, a fanatical *Chicago* sports fan. He put '1957' on the blackboard as one of the pivotal years in modern history. We were stumped. 1957? Eisenhower's presidency? The debut of *Leave it to Beaver*? Then Brother Weilatz wrote, "The year the Chicago White Sox won the pennant!"

He was one of a kind. We'd always laugh when he'd say, "Repeat after me: 'Repetition is the key to learning.' Then he'd smile and say, "Repeat."

A man of humor and joy, Brother was at the same time, deeply spiritual. Shortly before graduation, he surprised me with a question.

"Rzeppa, have you ever thought about becoming a Christian Brother?"

I was taken aback. I'd been accepted at Boston University and the Brotherhood wasn't on my radar. He persisted.

"You're a quarterback. You're a leader. If you give the Brothers a shot, other guys will follow you."

I was honored that he thought of me in these terms, but I just didn't feel called. The Christian Brothers of Ireland was not the brotherhood I was looking for.

BALL HANDLING

I wanted to play college basketball. Devoid of scholarship offers, I was determined to make it as a walk-on at Boston University.

To prepare, I employed the *Think and Grow Rich* philosophy of Napoleon Hill. One of Hill's points was to set a Definite Major Purpose. The Purpose and the way to achieve it should be written out and repeated aloud every morning upon rising and every night before retiring. Shades of Brother Weilatz.

I was all in. Full of determination, I wrote, "I, Zip Rzeppa, will become a major college basketball player. I will accomplish this goal by working endlessly to improve my skills, getting myself in tremendous physical condition, and playing with all-out passion. I will accomplish this goal at Boston University."

So I trained like a maniac for weeks. I ran mile after mile along the Charles River. I ran up and down the 70 steps of BU's football stadium, and then up and down the next section, and then up and down the next, and the next. I went to Boston's toughest playgrounds and competed against the top players. By the time tryouts rolled around, I was ready to become BU's version of Notre Dame's "Rudy"—undersized and lacking in talent, but full of passion and determination.

I was helped immeasurably by a long-outdated rule in effect back then: all college freshmen were limited to playing on the *freshman* team. So in my first year, all I had to do—all I was *eligible* to do—was to make the freshman squad.

The best freshman at BU was easy to spot. Kenny Boyd was 6-foot-5 and blessed with incredible talent, speed and jumping ability. As a senior in high school in Frederick, Maryland, Kenny *averaged* 29 points and 20 rebounds.

Apart from his spectacular talent, the thing that stood out about Kenny was his demeanor. He was so quiet that we hardly ever heard him speak. He let his game do the talking.

Unlike Kenny, I had to outwork and outhustle everyone else. My best skill was shooting from long range. Unfortunately, the three-point line didn't exist, so the coach was hardly excited to see this pint-sized guard throwing up heaves from 25 feet. It annoyed me that he termed my above-average range "a low-percentage shot."

Anyway, against all odds, I made the freshman team. I'll never forget the day of our first game. We were on a chartered bus to play the University of Maine. As evening fell, the darkened silence of the long bus ride was suddenly interrupted by the singing voice of Kenny Boyd. He sounded *exactly* like the lead singer of the Chi-Lites! He was singing their mega-hit, "Oh Girl."

This man who rarely spoke was filling the air with a mellow soprano voice that resonated off the roof of the bus. The rest of us instinctively jumped in, singing harmony. When we got to the chorus, there was Kenny, rising into the aisle, belting it out. Kenny moved on to another Chi-Lites hit, "Have You Seen Here." And again, the rest of us were eager to sing back up.

Kenny, our *silent* leader on the court, was bringing us closer together with his *pipes* on the bus. In case you're wondering, I was one heck of a harmonizer on those road trips.

Displaying the team nickname which struck fear into the hearts of all opponents

QUICK HANDS

After amazing my friends by making the freshman team, I decided I was going to make *varsity* my sophomore year.

Back in Detroit for summer break, I stepped up my training to almost inhuman, death-defying levels. I competed many a summer night on the playgrounds of the inner city, where oftentimes I was the only white player on the court. My friends thought I was asking for trouble, but I relished the fact that if you could play the game, color didn't matter. I would push myself to the limit, and then cover my car seat to protect the old leather interior from the saltwater pouring from every inch of my sweat-soaked body.

The playground games were rough, and occasionally tempers got short. There were no referees around, so the players had to settle the score amongst themselves. This usually worked out okay, but in one particular game, this big, tall, somewhat older guy said he was fouled, and his opponent claimed that he wasn't. Well, the disagreement escalated to the point where the big guy stormed off the court. Another player replaced him, and the game resumed. Ten minutes later, the big guy returned—with a shotgun.

"You want to say you didn't foul me now?" he asked.

That was the only time I ever hoped our team would lose—so I could get off the court and get outta there!

I took a job as a busboy at Uncle John's Pancake House. Each morning, my dad or my brother would drive me to work at 7:00 am. I'd hide my basketball in the back of the kitchen. When I got off, I'd dribble the ball home, a distance of four miles, to improve my ball handling.

I must have shot a million jump shots at the basket on our neighbors' driveway, and on any playground I could find. Many a night, long after the sun had set and I had survived the intense battles on the steaming asphalt of the inner city, I'd drive over to my high school track and run two or three miles in the dark.

Nevertheless, when I returned to BU, I was a longshot to make varsity.

A week before preseason practice began, all candidates for the squad had to run three miles in less than twenty minutes. I shocked myself when I turned in the second-fastest time. When we hit the court, I played with toughness and passion, and took delight in harassing the bigger, stronger, faster scholarship players. I played as if my life depended on it.

One day, the coach gave us a break from the monotony of the rigorous daily practice routine. He split us into three-man teams, and paired us up to play full-court games, with the first team to five baskets staying to face the next challengers. I was teamed with Kenny Boyd and a struggling forward whose name, Sweetwater Brock, was more exciting than his game.

Naturally, everyone expected Kenny to lead us offensively. But surprisingly, Kenny spent time setting picks for me and acting as a decoy. My best skill, shooting, came into focus. I made four shots in a row, and then Kenny's basket clinched the victory. Next!

Amazingly, the same scenario played out again and again. We won game after game until the coach called off practice.

As we walked off the court, Kenny said to me, "Great job!"

I responded, "Kenny, I'm just trying to make the team."

He looked me in the eye and said, "If you keep playing like that, you'll be *starting!*"

My limited skills soon brought me back down to earth, but I *made the team!* I had achieved my goal. I had become a varsity college basketball player.

I became pals with a fellow walk-on, Gerald McClellan. He was a slender African-American from rural Kentucky, and next to me, he was the shortest guy on the squad. It was a rare occurrence when either of us got off the bench. But we were the kings of the pre-game meal.

Back in the early '70s, carb-loading wasn't a big deal. Our usual diet was a big, juicy steak and a baked potato. Since Gerald and I knew our chances of actually *playing* were slim, the *pre-game meal* became the highlight of our day. We were always the last two guys to finish eating, which brought ridicule from our teammates.

But Gerald would wave his fork with a flourish and say, "Hey man! You gotta savor the flavor!"

Sophomore year, I only played in two games, but one was at the famed Boston Garden on the same parquet wood floor where Bill Russell and the mighty Celtics won 11 world championships in 13 seasons. We were playing Harvard, and we were behind by about 20 points, which was when my heart would start racing, because I knew I had a chance to actually play. When the coach put me in, we were taking the ball out of bounds, underneath the other team's basket. I was the trigger man. The ref blew his whistle and handed me the ball. Well, my eyes grew wide as my pal Gerald made a perfect cut off a screen and charged, unimpeded, toward the basket. I threw him a perfect bounce pass and he laid the ball up and in.

I'll never forget the thrill of racing back on defense on the precious parquet of the most famous basketball arena in the nation, having assisted on a basket in a major college basketball game.

After the season, I received my varsity letter at the official Boston University Basketball Banquet. Where did they hold the event? The Playboy Club. Like, they couldn't find any other place in Boston to have it? Now, I was as curious as the rest of the guys to see the Bunnies squeezed into their little outfits, but I was too embarrassed to tell my parents back in Detroit that they brought us there. My mom would have thought that Hugh Hefner was the emcee.

I could have made the team as a walk-on for two more years, but I figured future employers wouldn't exactly drool because I spent *four* seasons clapping my hands on the BU bench. I reduced my hooping to the BU intramural league where in my senior year, I helped our squad make it to the University championship game.

In case you're wondering, Kenny Boyd averaged more than 20 points a game over his varsity career, and then played briefly for the Jazz in the NBA.

Gerald McClellan became an attorney. I like to imagine that when he's wining and dining clients, at least once in a while he still advises, "Hey, man! You gotta savor the flavor!"

Kenny Boyd, back row, 3rd player from left; Gerald and me,
kneeling side-by-side, far right

THE HANDS OF FRIENDSHIP

On my first day at BU, I met the best friend of my college years, Bill Nussbaum. Bill was a tall New Yorker, a passionate crusader for justice with a defiant spirit expressed in hair down to his shoulders and the occasional wearing of overalls. He was proud of his Jewish heritage and railed against past and current persecutions of the Jews, but he had no interest in practicing the religion. As an agnostic, Christianity made no sense to Bill, which made our theological discussions quite interesting.

Bill was extremely bright and possessed a sharp wit. We shared a passion for writing and a great love of sports, although with different allegiances. We discussed and debated everything including religion and politics, openly sharing—and shying away from nothing. Whether agreeing or disagreeing, we always respected each other. It was a friendship to be cherished.

We were free spirits, each looking to experience with exuberance all that life had to offer through the backdrop of college. We dissected the lectures of our esteemed journalism profs, wrote for the university newspaper, shared meals in the cafeteria, and watched football, hockey, and hoops on the black-and-white TV in my dorm room. I was one of the few students who had a TV.

Aside from our religious differences, our greatest disagreements were over music. As a proud Detroiter, I was a fanatical lover of Motown, remaining ever true to the artists, writers, and musicians who spawned a genre that flourished in the '60s and into the '70s. Bill was a Big Apple boy attuned to the East Coast folk/rock sounds of James Taylor, Carole King, Joni Mitchell and others.

I tried in vain to convince Bill of the superiority of the lyrics, harmonies, and style of The Temptations, Diana Ross and the Supremes, The Four Tops, Marvin Gaye, Smokey Robinson and the Miracles, and Stevie Wonder, all of whom lived in Detroit. I'd play "My Girl" and "Ain't Too Proud to Beg" and couldn't understand Bill's reserved response. At least he listened. In turn, when Bill played his favorites—I would mock the compositions as inferior to Motown.

I acted like a jerk. And this kind of attitude revealed one of my great faults. I believed that whatever I thought was right or best or superior, was *in fact*, the way things were. In my arrogance, I did not see that I had a "God complex"—believing that I knew it all. I'm still not sure how Bill Nussbaum not only tolerated me, but remained my very close friend.

Anyway, my infatuation with Motown almost cost me my life when the Jackson 5, starring a very youthful Michael Jackson, came to Boston.

I had seen them the previous summer in Detroit as the closing act at an amazing event, a fundraiser for Detroit's greatest boxer, the legendary Joe Louis. Louis had reigned as heavyweight champion of the world for 12 years, longer than anyone in history, but the IRS and crooked managers had combined to take away all the money he had ever made. He was in failing health, in debt, and had been reduced to working as a greeter at a casino in Las Vegas.

When Berry Gordy, the founder and president of Motown Records, heard about Joe's plight, he ordered his superstars to do a benefit show at Cobo Arena. I'll never forget it. They brought Joe Louis into the arena in a wheelchair, and sat him up front. Bill Cosby flew in from the east coast to emcee. The Tempts and the Tops and Smokey and Marvin all rocked the place, and then 9-year-old Michael Jackson and his older brothers took the stage. Little Michael *electrified* the crowd. I watched from the balcony with tears in my eyes, so proud that Motown had come out to support its champ when life had knocked him to the mat.

Months later, I took public transportation to see the show in Boston. The Jackson 5 dazzled, especially Michael, who had just turned 10. As the lights came up, I headed to the subway which is connected to the Garden by an indoor tunnel about 25 feet wide. Unhappily, with 16,000 people heading for the exits, people with evil in their hearts saw an opportunity to take advantage.

Walking toward me in the tunnel was a group of five young black men, and they weren't the Jackson 5. I became apprehensive when I noticed that one was carrying a tire iron. Before I could think further, they were upon me. One asked for my wallet and before I could respond, I collapsed to the ground as the tire iron crashed down on my skull. One of the men reached into my pocket, grabbed my wallet, emptied it of a $20 bill, and threw the wallet in front of my face, which was a couple of inches from the dirty cement floor and a small pool of my blood. The group stared at me, and I knew I had no way out. The tire iron wielder raised his weapon and I covered my head, leaving my back fully exposed.

For some reason, the man decided not to follow through. He brought the tire iron to his side, and the young hoodlums moved on, looking for other prey. Bleeding and shaking on the cement, I got up, covered my wound with a handkerchief, and staggered into the subway station. I rode the Green Line back to campus, and headed to the infirmary, where the attendant closed the gash under a large lump that would take weeks to heal.

I was aware that if the culprit had blasted my head again, or had brought the iron to my spine, I could have spent the rest of my life brain-damaged or paralyzed. Only through the grace of God did he decide to move away, and only through God's grace did I *not* find myself further engaged in a brutal 5-on-1 confrontation.

Happily, I had many more pleasant moments at ancient Boston Garden. Freshman year, Bill Nussbaum and I applied for part-time jobs as vendors. Bill told the food service boss of his experience as a vendor at New York's Madison Square Garden. I lied and said that I had been a vendor at Cobo Arena. Well, at least I'd *been* to Cobo Arena.

This was the age of Bobby Orr, Phil Esposito, and some of the greatest Bruins teams ever. Lucky for us, we got hired. Now, if a Bruins fan ever missed a goal because some kid vendor was standing in front of him, there would have been a homicide at the Garden, so we were only allowed to sell Cokes before the game and between periods. The rest of the time, we sat on the Garden steps and watched *almost all of every game for free*. Life was good!

Well, it was until we got fired. During a brief downturn in their history, the Boston Celtics were *not* selling out every game. Thus, Bill and I were summoned to work at only a handful of NBA games. When my beloved Detroit Pistons came into town, I convinced Bill to go to the game. We were not scheduled to work, but we flashed our vendor badges and got in. We were sitting in some empty seats, enjoying the action, when the boss man approached. Well aware that we were not on the work schedule, he confiscated our badges and fired us on the spot. It was one of the darkest days of my young life.

Bill and I bounced back by getting unpaid positions doing sports-casts at the campus radio station, WTBU. The station was run by students, and unless you were within two blocks of the dorms, all you could hear was static. But it was there that I fell in love with the imme-diacy of radio. I was a good writer and my energy and humor over-came the shortcomings of my *unusual* broadcasting voice. In junior year, I became the station's sports director. Senior year, I did the color commentary of Boston University football and hockey games, along-side fellow student, Rick Benjamin, who did the play-by-play. Rick went on to become a distinguished local television anchorman who worked in San Antonio and Raleigh, among other places.

Of course, only a handful of people were listening to our tiny station, but that didn't matter to me. I was behind the microphone, and gaining experience. I pretended that we were being heard by *millions*.

Along the way, Nussbaum dropped broadcasting to study law. He became the youngest federal prosecutor to try rape and murder cases in Washington, DC, and then spent many years as a partner at the second biggest law firm in the nation's capital. We're still friends.

OFFERING MY HAND

To other students on campus, I probably looked like a big success. I had achieved my goal of becoming a college basketball player, and I was a standout on the campus radio station. But interiorly I was hungering for something else. The one area in my life where I was an utter failure—was romance.

My high school experience with women consisted of one date that ended with no kiss. I was too shy to go for it. So when I arrived at Boston University, where 55% of the student population was female, I was all but salivating. But one problem remained: this energetic basketball playing, budding sports broadcaster became paralyzed in the presence of an attractive woman. So I took the same approach toward women that I took toward sports—passionate, focused, and determined to get beyond my natural shortcomings, and score.

But the disaster of the Creedence Clearwater Revivial contest exemplified my continuing failure to get dates. I defaulted to pornography, and for two years it became the sad, lonely substitute for what I really wanted.

Mercifully, things changed at the beginning of my junior year. Hungering for more than porn on my first day back at school, I knelt down and asked God to send me a girlfriend. That evening, a bunch of friends asked me to go to a mixer. When we got there, I was dismayed that the crowd was small. To try to get things going, the disc jockey offered a free drink to any guy who would ask a girl to dance. So, I walked over to this petite, attractive brunette, and I asked her.

She replied, "Do you want to dance, or do you just want the free drink?" I thought that was cute, but being the dork that I was, I had to think through my reply. Finally I stammered, "Um, maybe both?"

Fortunately, she didn't blow me off. And later that night, as our crowd walked back to the dorm, I was the only guy walking with a girl. It was the new highlight of my social life.

The girl's name was Abby. Our differences were obvious. I was male, she was female, and I *loved* that. I was strong-willed, sports-obsessed, and competitive. She was thoughtful, sweet, and tender. I was a Catholic boy from Detroit who still went to Mass every Sunday. She was a non-practicing Jewish girl from New York who had spent the last two years in Israel, going to the University of Tel Aviv at the insistence of her parents. I was pursuing a career in journalism; she was majoring in occupational therapy.

Well, Abby and I became very close, very fast. At last, I was in the relationship game. We were both willing and eager players. Pursuing passion with Abby was exciting but there was a big difference from the selfish experience of porn. Now there was another person involved, and if I indulged my appetite, there was a chance of a *third* person making the scene. This terrified me, but Abby told me there were only a few days a month she could get pregnant and not to worry about it.

Many students at BU were having sex, but not many did what I did *after* sex. I went to confession. I felt cleansed of my sin, forgiven. I had resolved "to sin no more," but my resolution was overcome by the seductiveness of Abby and my own lustful habits. I had moved from porn to a "relationship," but inside, it strangely felt like the same thing.

I achieved the goal but somehow it felt hollow. I was empty. I was still hungry, hungering for something else.

Abby was a slam-dunk for me, but I was starting to sense that, as with porn, getting points on the board with Abby wasn't enough.

KNUCKLING DOWN

At BU's highly-ranked journalism school, I had a number of terrific professors. My favorite was Timothy Cohane who served for many years as the sports editor of Look Magazine, a major publication in the 1940s and '50s.

Old Tim was Old School. If you were more than five minutes late for the start of class he would slam the door and not let you in. He would teach the class in the tone of a football coach, barking, "Rewrite! Rewrite! Rewrite!" "Verbosity is the enemy!" "I never want anyone in here to write: 'Needless to say.' If it's needless to say, then why the hell say it?!"

I shared four years of communications classes with a long-haired boy from New York, Howard Stern. Yep, *that* Howard Stern. As you may guess, Howard wasn't exactly sitting in the front row of the class, hanging on the professor's every word. In the vernacular of the times, he was a free thinker, and I respected that. He danced to a different drummer, and outside of class, he ran with his own posse. Somehow I wasn't invited.

In the final semester of my senior year, I mistakenly enrolled in a *graduate school* course in Broadcast Journalism. I don't know how the admissions folks failed to catch the mistake. Maybe they were just glad my tuition was paid. Talk about serendipity! The course brought me into contact with a student destined to become my lifelong friend. His name was Bill O'Reilly. Yep, *that* Bill O'Reilly.

The class was taught by John Lord, a distinguished television producer for the BBC. John gave us a glimpse of all aspects of a newscast. We performed the duties of director, producer, audio engineer, and graphics coordinator, as well as the on-air broadcast positions, in mock 30-minute TV productions. Fortunately, none of our efforts were seen by actual viewers.

I was thrilled when I was assigned to do the sports segment. I diligently prepared, ripping stories off the old wire service machines which pumped out the news of the world in staccato fashion. I enthusiastically wrote my script.

When showtime arrived, I was ready. Or so I thought. The news segment ended, and the student anchorman tossed me my cue. As the camera focused on me, I opened my mouth to begin—but no sound came out. My voice was frozen! I remember reaching my hand up to my throat, as if I could physically massage the words into emerging. I was stunned to hear my fellow students erupt in raucous laughter.

Well, my paralysis lasted about two seconds, although it seemed like two hours, and my voice miraculously returned. So I looked straight into the camera and did a damn-near-perfect, powerful presentation of the sports news. And again I was stunned, this time to hear the entire class burst into spontaneous applause. Oh, the agony and the ecstasy! Such experiences under Professor Lord gave me confidence that someday I might make it.

SLIPPING THROUGH MY FINGERS

In the midst of my academic progress, my inordinate passion for pleasure and thrills flared up, this time in the form of gambling. It started with a seemingly harmless trip to a local racetrack. When some fellow students and I got lucky and won, our forays evolved into a three-times-a-week habit.

When our luck at the track soured, we began betting on sports events through a local bookie operation instead. Our connection was a guy who looked almost young enough to be a student. He would take our bets each week over the phone and then we'd meet him face-to-face each Tuesday to collect our cash if we won—or to pay up if we lost.

Deep into the final semester of my senior year, we had pretty much broken even. This didn't satisfy us. One night in March we decided we'd win big on the NCAA basketball tournament.

We bet on a total of six games. It's all but impossible to lose them all, but we did. My friends had each bet 100 to 200 dollars per game, so if you multiply by six, they had lost quite a sum. Being a little more daring, or stupid, I had bet *500* dollars per game, so my losses totaled $3,000. In 1974, that was a lot of bucks.

Unlike my friends, I knew I could not go home and ask for money, because my parents did not have it. My only hope was to bet some more, and win back the money. I called our bookie connection.

"Sorry, kid. You and your pals are down a lot of scratch. No more bets until you pay up. We'll see you Tuesday."

I gulped. I was frantic. I had to come up with $3,000 by Tuesday. In a moment, it came to me: *Las Vegas!*

In desperation, I scraped up some money and jumped on a plane headed for the Sunset Strip. It was not exactly a smooth flight. The wind stream over the mountains exceeded 100 miles an hour, and the plane started to shake violently. I was sure the plane was going to crash. I *knew* it. I was going to die, and I was going to go to hell because of my stupid gambling.

But somehow the pilot brought the plane in, and there I was, at the betting window. I had borrowed $500 from my reluctant friends out of the money they had secured from their parents. My strategy: bet the $500, win, and I'd have $1,000. Then bet the $1,000, win, and I'd have $2,000. Bet the $2,000, win, and I would have $4,000—$3,000 to pay off the bookies, and another $1,000 to fly home and pay off my friends.

All I had to do was pick three winners.

I put my $500 on Cincinnati to beat Boston College. BU had played against Boston College and I knew their team well. Little did I know that the star player on Cincinnati was injured. BC beat Cincy. I lost my bet.

I was broke. I mean, *completely* broke. All the betting windows in Vegas were of no use. I had no money. And I had to get back to Boston. I could have hitchhiked to the airport, but in my fragile mental state, I could see myself getting picked up by a serial killer who would chop up my body parts and scatter them on the side of the road. So I walked seven miles in the stifling Nevada heat, and arrived at the terminal, dripping wet with sweat. I called a friend whose mother was a travel agent, and mercifully, she wired me a plane ticket to get back to Beantown.

Tuesday came, and now I had to face the runner for the bookies. I confessed that I did not have the money.

Naturally, he was not pleased. "$3,000 is a lot of money, kid. You don't screw around with the people I'm working for. They'll break your legs."

I promised that I would somehow, someway, come up with the money to pay the debt. He arranged for me to have lunch with one of his "people."

I've had a lot of lunches, with a lot of *people*, but I'll never forget this one. The guy wore a black leather jacket. He had a swarthy complexion, punctuated by a sizeable scar on his cheek. I gulped, but thought to myself, o*kay, I can get through this.*

During lunch, Mr. Warmth snarled, "You're gonna give me the money you owe us."

At this point, I made the mistake of making a little joke. I gave him a little grin and said, "And, uh, what if I don't? What are you going to do? Kill me?"

Well, he leaned over the table until his face was about 6 inches from mine and growled, "Listen, punk. I got a knife in this jacket. I'll take you out in the street right now and cut you to pieces." Somehow, I got the impression he meant it.

So I changed my tone, and confessed that I didn't have *any* money, but I would get a job and pay every cent I owed. Snarly Man was not a big fan of that answer, but, through the grace of God, he didn't cut me into pieces.

HANDLING ADVERSITY

So now, two months away from graduation, I had to look for a job. I saw an ad from the Boston Ski and Sports Club. They needed someone to sell tennis lessons to beginners. The Sports Club's founder and boss, a young, bright, 30-something named Jerry Milden, took a liking to me and I was hired. So, for eight hours a day I'd sit on the phone and field calls from people responding to ads for tennis lessons. I was on commission, so I sold tennis lessons like nobody had ever sold them before. Jerry promoted me to Sales Manager.

Now I was making some money, but each week, I'd meet with the "rep" of the bookies and I'd cough up all the dough I made. Very, very painful.

While selling tennis lessons by day, I was studying at night, and finally graduated. My parents and youngest brother flew to Boston for the glorious occasion, and we celebrated. They asked me if I was coming home to Detroit. I told them I was doing well at the Boston Ski and Sports Club and was going to stay there, conveniently leaving out the part about how hit men might be looking for me if I stopped making payments and left town.

I had absolutely no money. A college gambling buddy let me sleep on his couch, but he wouldn't lend me anything. I remember putting water on my cereal because I didn't have any milk. I often ate one full meal a day. I became a big fan of macaroni and cheese, because a 59-cent box would fill my belly for hours. Another favorite was a huge order of chocolate chip pancakes at IHOP. Same reasoning.

I worked into the summer, week after week, and whittled my debt down from $3,000 to $1,000, but I just couldn't take this lifestyle. One of my colleagues at the Boston Ski and Sports Club had a bookmaker, so I thought, if I place *one* bet for $1,000 and win, all my debts are paid off, and I'm free. I've got a decent job, I'll *keep* the money that I make, eat three meals a day, and be able to afford a date.

I made my $1,000 bet. I lost. So now I owed the new bookmaker $1,000 which I didn't have, and I still owed $1,000 to the old bookies who had put me on the starvation diet.

I was despondent and desperate. I traipsed into Jerry Milden's office and gave him a total confession. Jerry was caught off guard. I was hoping he might advance me some money to pay off my debts, at least in part. He looked me in the eye and said, "These are the kind of people you don't want to play around with, Zip." Then he paused and reached into his pocket. I held my breath.

"Here's 50 dollars. Get yourself a one-way bus ticket to some place like Arizona, and never come back again, and hope that they never find you."

I gulped. Not exactly the answer I was hoping for. But I couldn't blame Jerry. I had made my bed, and I had to sleep in it. I clumped back to my friend's apartment, packed up my belongings, and scarfed a couple of twenties from him as a going-away gift.

I ordered a cab to pick me up the next day at work. I walked in to say goodbye to all of my colleagues, none of whom knew that any of this was going on, except for the guy who had referred me to his bookie, and he was damn mad at me.

Suddenly, Jerry called me into his office. He said, "Listen, you've made some terrible mistakes. But you're a good kid, and you're doing a great job here. I'm gonna help you out."

With that, he made a call to an attorney friend of his. I didn't know who the guy was, but I got the idea he wielded a lot of power. Jerry asked for the phone number of the first bookie. Jerry conferenced the bookie in with his attorney friend, who gave the bookmaker hell. He said, "My man here's been working his nuts off, and all the money has been going to you, pal. Well, we're gonna change the arrangement. He's gonna make much *smaller* payments until his debt is paid off, because we are honorable people."

My mouth dropped open as the bookie started to object. The attorney cut him off and chirped, "Well, there's another option, I could put you out of business," at which point the bookie backed down.

He said, "Okay, okay. Uhhhh, how much a week is your guy gonna pay us?" I almost fell out of my chair when Jerry said, "We're gonna make it 10 bucks a week." I wish I could have seen the bookie's face.

He shouted, "It'll take him a *lifetime* to pay back a thousand bucks!"

The prosecutor intoned, "Consider the alternative, pal!" and the deal was done. Jerry said he would pay off my $1,000 debt to the second bookie, and I could pay him back at $100 a week. I had been bailed out and kept alive by a very generous man.

I paid Jerry back within weeks. As for the original bookies, I think they got tired of making the weekly trip to collect my $10 bill, because the collection man said, "Look kid, just give me a 100 bucks next week and we'll call it square." I happily obliged.

I never made another bet in my life.

A new book by Napoleon Hill stated that "All money that is not earned is evil," that in the free enterprise system, we provide a service and are compensated accordingly. I saw that gambling was a *something-for-nothing* endeavor. What was I *giving* in return for a particular horse winning a race or a team winning a game? Nothing! Surely, I was risking my money, but I wasn't providing *anything* for *anyone* other than the racetrack folks or the bookies.

I contemplated this while sitting on the grass in Boston Common. I knew God had blessed me with above average intelligence, good health, a college education, creativity, imagination, and energy. I decided right then and there—I would use my gifts in service, in exchange for any money that I would ever make for the rest of my life. As I sat there—dead broke—I looked up at a swanky, 40-story apartment building and said to myself, "I can become a good enough broadcaster to live there someday. I'll do it by using my gifts."

But before I could start, the New England winter blew in, and I needed to make extra money to visit my parents in Detroit for

Christmas. So I got a temporary part-time job—playing Santa Claus. I thought it was a great idea. I was wrong. It was *the worst two-week job of my life.*

This wasn't the typical, cushy Santa position where you sit in a warm, cozy mall and hold wide-eyed toddlers on your knee. This job was *outside!* I was paid to walk in front of the 40 stores of a large Boston strip mall, ringing a hand bell and proclaiming, "Ho, Ho, Ho!"

There were problems right from the start. For one thing, I was rock-hard lean, and Santa has to be fat. One pillow prop wouldn't do. I needed two. Which would have worked fine if I was sitting down, but I had to be walking. Costume malfunction was a recurring problem. Then there was the weather. The temperature was a few degrees below *freezing my butt off,* and the contract said I had to walk for 30 minutes before I could enter a store for a 5-minute break.

The day a big snowstorm hit, there was hardly anybody at the strip mall. I was happy, as I figured I'd spend more time inside. But no! I became the holiday hostage of desperate retailers frantic to stay in the black during the white-out. They whipped me like the hind reindeer on Santa's sleigh, and insisted I *go out into the street,* and bell-ring and "Ho, Ho" to let people know they were still open. At the end of the gig, I had to peel the frozen black patent leather Santa boots off my feet. Somehow, frostbite didn't claim any of my toes.

THE GOLDEN TOUCH

The following spring, I made a move to start my broadcasting career. I approached Steve Meterparel, who hired the announcers for Boston University's football and hockey games on the Beacon Sports Network.

I applied along with my friend and fellow BU grad, Mike Paley.

Our only experience was our unpaid work at the tiny university station, but hey, we *had* broadcast BU sports! We made an elaborate presentation to Meterparel, and to our joy and surprise, he hired us! The key was our acceptance of a salary of $40 per game, a *wee bit below* what seasoned broadcasters made. We didn't care. We were professional broadcasters!

The BU football program was so weak that a few years later, the school dropped the sport, but broadcasting BU hockey was at the other end of the spectrum. The Terriers were perennial contenders to win the national championship.

Our favorite hockey players were Ricky Meagher and his close friend, Mike Eruzione. Paley and I would go wild when they hit the ice. Ricky and Mike were small in stature, but the instant they jumped over the boards, they skated like madmen. Their fire and emotion was unmatched, and they often came up with big goals in crunch time.

Eruzione grew up in Winthrop, about 10 miles from campus. His spirited parents listened to the road games. Mike's mom once told me, "You love Mike almost as much as we do!"

The 1975-76 season was unforgettable as BU skated its way through the NCAA tournament. Paley and I almost lost our voices when the Terriers advanced to college hockey's version of the Final Four.

The appropriately dubbed *Frozen Four* took place that year in St. Louis. In the national semifinals, BU was matched against the Minnesota Golden Gophers, coached by Herb Brooks. Brooks was so tough, we nicknamed him "Mr. Iron Pants."

In an extremely hard-fought game, the Terriers fell to the Golden Gophers, 4-2. Paley and I fought back tears in the broadcast booth. It was a long, sad bus ride with Eruzione, Meagher, and the rest of the players back to the hotel. The dream of winning a national champion-ship had ended.

But Eruzione got a chance to go after a bigger prize.

Four years later, a determined group of amateurs and college players banded together under the watchful eye of *Team USA Coach* Herb Brooks in the 1980 Winter Olympic Games in Lake Placid. I was among tens of millions of Americans who went crazy when team captain Mike Eruzione scored the winning goal against the seemingly unbeatable Russian "professionals" in what many consider to be the greatest and most exciting upset in the history of the Olympic Games.

THUMBS UP

As much as I loved being the voice of BU sports, I couldn't survive on 40 bucks a game, so I came up with a brilliant idea to syndicate a three-minute radio show. I bought myself a high quality audio tape recorder which my brother cemented into a metal brief-case. I set out to interview top sports stars, edit the tapes, and sell the shows to radio stations.

I began living on buses. I'd ride the Greyhounds for days to get to major sports events. There were side effects. Man, you haven't lived until you've shaved with a razor in a downtown bus station restroom.

But sometimes I discovered unexpected pleasures. On an all-nighter from the Midwest to Boston, I wound up sitting next to a young redhead. She stood out among the cast of midnight bus riders like Pavarotti at a karaoke contest.

I told her I was a radio sportscaster, and she seemed impressed. She told me she was a lion tamer, and I was *really* impressed. In actuality, she traveled to malls to put on shows with carefully trained lion cubs. Children came running to see the show. After a few lion tricks, she would snap pictures of the kids and cubs, and sell them at outrageous prices to the parents. Clever gig!

Obviously, we were kindred spirits, two young people crazy enough to ride buses all over the country. A nine-to-five job wasn't our style. As the Greyhound rolled through the darkness, she put her head on my shoulder, and fell asleep. In my nomadic life, moments of romance were rare, so this was pure sweetness. I began dreaming of capturing the lion tamer. When we hit Boston in the wee hours of the morning, we shared a cup of coffee at the bus station—but the 'hounds ended up taking us in different directions. Talk about a short-lived romance.

THE WINNING TOUCH

I wasn't looking for love anyway. I was determined that nothing was going to stop me from interviewing America's sports superstars. The buses got me to major stadiums where I'd call a public relations big-wig and tell him I was the host of a nationally syndicated radio program. I wasn't lying—the program just hadn't hit the airwaves yet! Somehow, the PR folks always bought it. I wound up with media passes to everything.

I remember busing to Buffalo for the Stanley Cup finals between the Sabres and the Flyers. I crashed the Flyers' hotel early in the afternoon. The players were nowhere in sight, but as I wandered around, I found future hockey Hall of Famer Fred "The Fog" Shero, the team's head coach, sunning himself poolside. What luck!

"The Fog" nickname originated through a series of drinking stories, but that day Shero was sipping a can of Coke. I had never met him, but I knew all about him. He was the only NHL coach who played the violin, read Dickens, and quoted Shakespeare. He rarely yelled at his players, communicating instead by leaving notes in their lockers.

As I approached him, I had no fear that this Renaissance man would throw me in the pool, but I didn't know how he would engage me. Naturally, I was toting my metal briefcase with the hidden tape recorder inside. To my delight, Fred consented to an interview.

What an interview it was! This legendary coach had no idea who I was, but he completely opened up and described in detail the unique system he developed to turn his so-called Broad Street Bullies into champions. It was emotional, heartfelt, inside stuff.

That night, Fred coached the Flyers to their second consecutive Stanley Cup title. And I put together one heck of a radio show. No one ever knew that "The Fog" did the interview in his bathing suit.

I loved putting together radio programs like that. But despite Greyhound's generous discount rates, I was going broke traveling across the country. I couldn't get enough radio stations to buy the programs to make a living.

That's when another idea popped into my head. If I became a local *television* sportscaster, all the radio stations in the area would carry my radio show, and we could expand from there. Terrific! All I needed now was to get on TV!

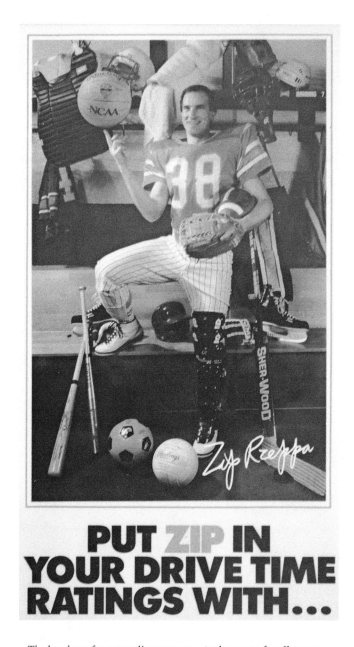

The brochure for my radio program…truly a man for all seasons.

A TOUCH OF EXCITEMENT

This was the 1970s. There were only three network-affiliated TV stations in each city: CBS, NBC, and ABC. The Fox Network was years away, as were cable, satellite, hulu, and cellphones. Al Gore hadn't even *thought* of inventing the Internet. So the competition for TV jobs was fierce.

I sent letters and resumes to 150 local TV stations. Ian Pearson, the news director of the CBS station in tiny Fort Wayne, Indiana, responded. I drove to Fort Wayne and auditioned. Ian said he'd get back to me. A few days later, he called.

"You're the best we've auditioned, and I'm going to offer you the job, but you are probably not going to want to take it."

I'm thinking, *there's no way in the world I'm going to turn down a job on TV!*

He explained, "The position is only one night a week, on Saturdays, and I can only pay you 40 bucks a week."

My heart sank. I was doing the BU broadcasts for 40 bucks a *game*. This was a demotion. 40 bucks *a week*?! But I needed to get on TV. "I'll take it!" I blurted. I'd worry about making a living later.

So I packed up my few earthly belongings, and moved to Fort Wayne. Ian was only 27-years-old, and he was good to me. He let me sleep on his couch while I looked for an apartment—and an outside job to supplement my meager paycheck.

I'll never forget my first television sportscast. After training for a couple of weeks, I made my debut on a Saturday night in the spring of 1976. My heart was pounding at about a million beats a minute.

I did the sportscast pretty well, no fumbles, no mistakes, and breathed a sigh of relief. As soon as we were off the air, I ran to look at the tape. I only wanted to know one thing: was I too *ugly* to make it as a television sportscaster?

I knew I would never look like a movie star. As I watched the tape, I concluded that I looked 'passable.' I was happy with 'passable.' There was hope!

The following week, a couple of touring golf pros came to Fort Wayne to play a friendly 18-hole match for a local charity. This was a pretty big deal, as pro golfers didn't exactly *gravitate* to Fort Wayne. The match was on a weekday, and our Monday-through-Friday sports anchor asked me to substitute for him, so he could hang with the golfers, and enjoy the charity dinner.

In the hot summer sun, I walked with the media for the first few holes of the match. The weekday sports guy offered me a beer. I remember having two. I don't think it was three. When I returned to the station to prepare for my sportscast, I felt a little buzz. Uh-oh.

Here I was about to do the *weeknight* sportscast for the first time, and to be on TV for only the second time in my life, and I was all but reeling with light-headedness. I started chewing gum to take care of my breath. Why did I drink those beers?

Through the grace of God, I made it through the 6pm sportscast. And somehow, I managed to do an 11pm sportscast that the station general manager complimented me on the next day. But what if I had had one *more* beer? My TV career could have ended a week after it had begun.

Fort Wayne was only 125 miles from Indianapolis, so Ian and I got media passes to the Indianapolis 500. The passes got us into the pits, around the garages, anywhere we wanted. I must say, from the infield, *The Greatest Spectacle in Racing* looked like *The Greatest Spectacle in Drinking.*

Anyway, the engines roared, the flag dropped, the fans went wild, and we were having a great time. Then the rain came. Torrential rain. We were among hundreds of thousands of spectators who got drenched. The Indy 500 turned into the Indy 250, as the race was declared over. What a bummer!

As Ian and I drove back to Fort Wayne in the pouring rain, we consoled ourselves that for the rest of our lives, we could say we "covered" the Indianapolis 500.

UPHILL CLIMB

Shortly thereafter, I got a phone call from the boss of a TV station in Saginaw, Michigan, where I had auditioned a couple months earlier.

"I heard that you got a job, but we want to hire you. How much are you making in Fort Wayne?"

I couldn't tell him 40 bucks a week. "Well, right now, I'm just doing weekends, and um, some other stuff during the week, and um, uh…"

"Come up here to Saginaw. We've got a full-time job for you, with a salary of $15,000."

$40 a week versus $15,000 a year? Easy decision.

We set the start date a month out, so Ian Pearson could find a replacement for me. I didn't want to screw the guy who hired me, let me sleep on his couch, and went with me to the '500.'

In July of 1976, I drove my rented Ford Pinto six hours from Fort Wayne to WNEM-TV, the NBC-TV affiliate in the Flint-Saginaw-Bay City market. The viewing area covered about a quarter of the lower peninsula of Michigan.

I worked with some real characters in Saginaw. The weekday weathercaster, Jim Peyton, would sketch a drawing on an easel *while he was doing the weather*. A veritable meteorologist/artist. If it was cold, he might draw a polar bear with a scarf around its neck while he yammered about snow and dropping dew points. He'd always time it so that the second he finished the forecast, he'd finish the drawing. Then he'd say, "This one's going out to Maude in Port Huron."

Thousands of people sent in postcards, begging for Jim's art work, and they'd all tune in to see if they were the winner. A great gimmick. And very good for Jim's job security.

The weekend weathercaster, Chuck Waters, was a spirited, gray-haired man in his early 60s. Whenever he predicted that the overnight low would be below 10 degrees, which was fairly often, Chuck would always tell the viewing audience, "You better get your snuggies out tonight!" I'm not sure exactly how many viewers knew what snuggies were, but you can be sure the whole town was bundling up.

Chuck was a wild and crazy hockey fan, and Saginaw had a minor league team, the Saginaw Gears. The Gears were named in honor of the Saginaw Steering Gear factory, where it seemed about half the town worked, 24 hours a day, seven days a week, in three shifts. I don't want to say there wasn't much else to do during the frozen Saginaw winters, but the Gears had no trouble attracting fans. They averaged about 5,000 a game.

Chuck had season tickets right behind the visiting team's bench, and Mr. Weatherman, exhibiting amazing class, would pop out of his seat and scream obscenities at the opposing players and the referees.

This always created a stir. Half the fans would say, "Yeah, you go get 'em Chuck!" while the other half were screaming "Sit the hell down, Waters, I wanna see the game!" Only in Saginaw.

My boss was Marc Wesley, the sports director. He was happy to smoke his pipe and work in Saginaw for the rest of his life. I don't blame the guy. He had a comfortable life, a nice wife, and he was kind to me.

Marc loved to head to northern Michigan to shoot film of snow-mobile racing, a sport in which nobody had *any* interest, except for the racers and their girlfriends. I mean, standing outside in five-degree temperatures watching snowmobiles ain't exactly a *major spectator sport.* But the snowmobile racing association provided Marc with lots of free meals and all the booze he could drink, so it was a nice way for him to spend his weekends.

Working in Saginaw in the '70s was like working in TV's Dark Ages. When I went out to cover stories, I was my own camera man. I would set the old TV film camera on a tripod, turn the camera on, and then run around to the other side and interview athletes. Then I'd run back behind the camera to turn it off, because I was only allotted so much film. The term selfie hadn't been invented, but this was selfie on film.

I'd drive the film back to the TV station, go into the dark room, empty the film out of the camera into a dark bag, and after it was processed, I'd write, produce, and edit the film into my nightly sportscast. I didn't mind all of that, but the hours were long. I'd never leave the station until after midnight following the 11pm sportscast. Thus, many a night, I was driving home in the horrendous Michigan winter weather.

One night, I almost didn't *make* it home. The station was located in a cornfield. Literally. Three miles of two-lane highway led to the interstate. The fog was so thick that I was scared to death. I literally drove 5 miles-an-hour while *holding the driver's side door open* so I could see the center line. I was terrified that a driver coming the other way would take the car door off, and my arm with it. But if I closed the door, I feared drifting across the line. In the rare instance when a car came, I didn't see its headlights until it was three feet in front of me. It took me 45 minutes to go the three miles to the interstate.

HOLY HANDS

The highlight of the Saginaw social calendar was the first Saturday night of the month when this hot bluegrass band played the Holiday Inn. I was doing the 11pm sportscast so I could only catch the last set, between midnight and closing time. The star of the band was a terrific fiddle player. He'd resin up his bow and launch into action, his wand moving like lightning over the strings on the "Wabash Cannonball" and the "Orange Blossom Special." The packed crowd would hoot, holler, and chug.

Finding any kind of excitement on my nights off—Mondays and Tuesdays—was a major challenge. But God has amazing ways of working with us, and He used one particular Monday night to re-direct my entire life.

With little hope of finding a hot date, I was sitting in my apartment. There was a Bible on my coffee table. I never read it, but it was always there. For some reason, I decided to pick it up and read whatever I opened to. It happened to be 1 Corinthians 6:9-10, "Do not be deceived; neither fornicators, nor idolaters, nor adulterers, nor boy prostitutes, nor sodomites, nor thieves, nor the greedy, nor drunkards, nor slanderers, nor robbers will inherit the Kingdom of God."

This passage stunned me. I started to go through the sins. Idolatry? I wasn't about to worship the golden calf. Adultery? I never had sex with my friends' wives. My friends weren't even married. I did not indulge in any of the other things on the list—except for one—fornication. I wanted to make sure that was okay.

So I called up the rectory. There were two priests at my parish. One gave interesting homilies, the other one put people to sleep. I made an appointment with the interesting guy.

He was a Franciscan. We met outside the rectory on a pleasant summer day. I told him how I read 1 Corinthians 6 and I said, "Father, there's only one thing in there that bothers me—fornication."

He gave me a slight smile, and nodded. I said, "How can this passage say that the fornicators will not inherit the Kingdom of Heaven? If I have sex with a woman who is not married, a woman who consents, what's wrong with that?'"

He didn't give me a long answer, but he hit me with courageous clarity. "You can't do that. That's a mortal sin."

I can't describe how ticked off I was. I was 25-years-old and had only had sex with one woman in my life. But now, as I was getting over my social awkwardness and getting established in a *glamorous* career, I sensed that I was on the verge of increasing *opportunities*. I didn't want to hear about a ban on fornication.

But I trusted that this priest knew what was right, and would give it to me straight.

"Oh, man, Father," I moaned. "Wow. Oh, well," I said, pausing for a second to think, "I guess I'll just have to masturbate."

Father instantly responded, "Nope, you can't do that either. That's wrong, too."

Again, I was stunned. "No! Father, you're killing me!"

In actuality, what he was killing was the Evil One's deception that had made me believe that sex outside of marriage was okay.

I went home and spent time thinking about this. I was greatly attracted to women, and my mind moved very easily to sex. I *knew* that I would have plenty of chances to gratify my sexual desires. But that Biblical passage wouldn't go away. "The fornicators...will not inherit the Kingdom." I knew that God had established the Catholic Church and had empowered it to teach the truth, and I knew this priest had accurately imparted the Church's teachings.

So I was faced with one of the most major decisions of my life. I had three choices: I could commit sexual sins against the Church's teachings but still go to Mass and masquerade as a Catholic; I could quit the Church and do what I wanted to do; or I could *actually be* a Catholic and abide by God's laws.

I've always hated hypocrites, so I decided against choice number one. Choice number two was tempting, and my flesh ever so strongly desired that I go with that one. But while I was hardly a saint, my love for God and His Church wouldn't let me do that. I decided to go with choice number three.

And that choice changed my life forever.

I lost none of my interest in women. I simply changed from dating in the hope of having sex, to dating in the hope of finding a wife.

SLAPPED SILLY

One weekend I was out filming highlights of a gymnastics meet at Central Michigan University. I did an interview with the coach, a young, attractive, former outstanding college gymnast herself. Let's call her Jackie.

Well, I decided to ask Jackie out. CMU was about 45 miles away, but one day she drove to Saginaw and we had a pretty darn good time. I was filled with hope. Then she called and said she was leaving to take a position assisting the United States Olympic women's gymnastics team in northern California.

I was disappointed. We hadn't had enough time to see where our relationship might go, but I would have liked to have had the chance to find out. I was resigned that it was never going to happen.

Then one night, I got a call from Jackie. We were having a nice little chat when she suddenly asked me to come out to California to spend a weekend at her place.

Wow. Phew! Yes! Of course I wanted to go, and I was confident we'd keep it chaste. I booked a flight, which takes about four-and-half hours from Michigan, and arrived at the airport in a Bay Area fog. Who cares? This was my first trip to California. My reunion with Jackie. I was feeling great!

I called her when my flight arrived. She told me to rent a car and gave me directions to her house. She said she was going to introduce me to a friend of hers when I got there.

A friend? Whoa. Kind of strange. But hey, I was not only curious, I was even a little excited. I mean, it was too early to know how Jackie really felt about me, but I was certain that she thought of me as a good guy. Maybe she wanted me to fly out to meet a girlfriend of hers. Hey, I'd be open to that. I figured I was going to find out about Jackie, and if I wasn't to be with her, maybe I was to be with her friend.

So I jumped in the rental and drove to her house, singing, "I Wish They All Could Be California Girls." I was pumped, and ready for anything.

Well, almost.

As soon as I got to her house, Jackie and I exchanged a warm greeting. Then she said, "Come and meet my friend."

And her friend was not a woman. He was a man. And not just *any* man. He was her *boyfriend*. And the house we were in was *his*. She was living with him. He was the head coach of the United States Olympic wrestling team.

I was totally stunned. Speechless. Not to mention—*totally confused*. What the—?

A few thoughts popped into my spinning head, the first of which was, I'm not going to *fight* the United States Olympic Team wrestling coach. And then there was anger. Why would she do this to me? And then I had a moment of hope. Maybe she *does* have a girlfriend for me.

So I started glancing around the house. I avoided the gaze of the U.S. wrestling guru, and asked, "Uh, is anyone else joining us here?"

Jackie gave me this vapid smile and said, "No. It's just us."

I was baffled. I knew there *had* to be a reason she had me fly out to California, but I had no clue. I stammered, "So, uh, it's nice to be here." *Like hell it was.* "Um, uh, what are we gonna do?" I sure as hell didn't want this to get kinky.

Jackie gave me this little laugh. "We're so glad you're here, Zip. We're going to take you to a meeting tomorrow night."

"Um, a meeting? What kind of meeting?" *Could this possibly get any stranger?*

She said, "A business meeting."

"Huh. Um, a business meeting?" That didn't compute. "Uh, you know, I'm very happy being a sportscaster. I'm, uh, not really a business guy."

She answered, "Just go to bed and get a good night's sleep, and we'll show you what's happening at the meeting tomorrow night."

So I tried to sleep, but the weirdness and unanswered questions made it difficult, as did the fact that my little Jackie was upstairs sleeping with the U.S. Olympic team wrestling coach. I barely slept a wink.

Anyway, the next morning, the two of them took off, telling me to make myself at home until their return. *Right.* All I could do was desperately search for ways to kill time. This was years before cable TV and the Internet, so it was a challenge. I thought about snooping around the house, but I feared being placed in a hammerlock or a sleeper hold if the wrestling behemoth returned unexpectedly. Anyway, I didn't even *want* to snoop, because I was mad as hell at Jackie, and I hated the coach for no other reason than he was living with her.

So I spent the day reading a self-help book on how to accomplish great things, and eating health food stuff out of the fridge and pantry. Late in the afternoon, Miss Gymnastics and the Guru of Grappling arrived home, and almost immediately, we set off to go to the "business meeting."

They drove me to a nice private home, and introduced me to about 40 people, most of them couples. I still had no idea.

The meeting began. It was conducted by a yuppie guy in a sport coat who started writing numbers on a flip chart, set up on an easel.

Suddenly, I figured it out. To my horror, I realized—*I was at an AMWAY meeting!*

In case you don't know, AMWAY is—and I have to be careful here so I don't get sued—a kind of pyramid type deal where people sell soap and other products, and then get others to come in under them and sell the products, and then *they* get others to come in under *them*, and on and on, and everyone gets a cut from the sales.

So now I got the picture. My cute little gymnastics coach figured that as a TV sportscaster I was in a profession where loads of people would love to become "business partners" with me, and since I had a friendly, outgoing personality, I could convince a lot of people to jump in, and since I would come in under the group headed by Jackie and Mr. Wrestling, that they were going to make a lot of money.

This was the biggest shock of my life, to date. I could not believe that my perky gymnastics coach/buddy from Michigan had asked me to fly all the way across the country for *this!* So there I was, stuck in some stranger's home somewhere in California, with no way to escape, and with no option but to sit through this meeting. It was the longest 90 minutes of my life. I couldn't *wait* to leave the warmth of California and return to the frozen tundra of Saginaw.

POINTING THE WAY

I loved my job as a television sportscaster. It combined writing, producing, and performing. It was glamourous and fun, but I wanted to do it somewhere other than Saginaw. I was covering high school football, snowmobile races, Frisbee tournaments, free throw shooting contests, and possum hunts. What I *wanted* to cover was major league sports. I also wanted to make more than $15,000 a year in return for a 60-to-70-hour work week.

So on my summer vacation, I'd get in my eight-year-old Cadillac with the big fins and loud plaid interior that I bought from my dad, and I'd drive to TV stations in major league sports cities.

I called Ken Tiven, the news manager at KYW-TV in Philadelphia, and introduced myself. He agreed to take a look at my demo tape. I was filled with energy as I walked through the gleaming offices and studios of Channel 3 in the 4th biggest television market in the country. Ken had rocketed through the ranks at a very young age. I was 25 and he didn't look much older. I showed him a video of my very best sportscast in Saginaw.

As it ended, I said, "Well, what do you think?"

Ken didn't hesitate. "It's a rather bland, run-of-the-mill regurgitation of sports stories and scores."

My heart sank. I was crushed. I recovered enough to ask, "What do I have to do to work in a place like this?"

He got out of his chair, removed the tape, and handed it to me. He looked me in the eye and said, "You will likely be the ugliest sportscaster in any market in which you work. If you want to make it, you've got to be *different*."

So, I asked him what he meant by *different*. He told me about a sportscaster in Washington who did the sports like a comedian, and about a sportscaster in New York who ran exciting highlights back-to-back-to-back. He gave me another couple of examples and then said, "I've got to get to a meeting."

My time with Ken Tiven had lasted less than 15 minutes, but it would influence the rest of my career in TV.

I drove the Caddy back to Saginaw and began injecting humor into my broadcasts. I created "Zip's Zaps," in which I would mock athletes who did stupid things. "Zip's Tips" were my colorful predictions. "Zip's Trips" were entertaining takes on everyday sports stories. I pushed the envelope in countless ways—keeping what worked and throwing out what failed.

Then I put together a highlight reel of my most colorful stuff and sent it NBC-TV Vice-President and talent scout, Bill Slatterer, in Chicago.

Three days after I mailed the tape, Slatterer was on the phone. "I look at hundreds of sportscasters from all across the country," he said. "They are all good looking with good voices. In other words, they are all pretty much the same." He paused for a moment and then said, "But you are an *original*. I'm going to help you get a job in a bigger market."

CLIMBING THE LADDER

Slatterer recommended me to his longtime friend, Al Synder. Al had worked in Washington as a producer and had just been hired to manage the NBC-TV station in Cincinnati. Al loved my tape and made me an offer. At age 27, I was hired to do the Monday-through-Friday sportscasts at 5pm, 6pm, and 11pm, and the play-by-play of Cincinnati Bengals pre-season telecasts.

A few days before I went on the air, station management threw a gala cocktail party to introduce me to sponsors and media types. A huge screen dropped down to show highlights of my colorful antics. The tape drew a mixed reaction. Some applauded, others seemed to say, "They hired a crazy man!" Al Synder came up and put his arm around me.

"I was watching the bartender, Zip."

"The bartender?"

"He was laughing. He *loved* it. He's our audience!" I smiled. I had a feeling I might make it in Cincy.

But right off the bat, I almost got fired. On air, I blasted some athlete who made a stupid decision on the playing field, and it cost his team the game. I mocked him in a colorful, hilarious, dynamic commentary which I punctuated with the phrase, "What a schmuck!"

Five minutes after the broadcast, Snyder brought me into his office and slammed the door.

Al, who was Jewish, said, "Do you know what the word 'schmuck' means in Yiddish?"

I thought for a couple of seconds. "Um, it means idiot, fool, someone doing something stupid?"

Al glared at me. "It means—penis."

I was stunned. For a moment I couldn't speak. "You mean, I went on the air and called that guy a *penis?*"

"Yes."

I could see all the years it took me to get to a major league sports town going down the drain. "Am I fired?"

Al let me sweat for a couple of seconds, then said, "No. But don't *ever* use that word again."

I breathed a sigh of relief. Fortunately, I had more than schmuck-filled commentaries in my arsenal.

REACHING ACROSS BOUNDARIES

The year was 1981, and the sight of women sports reporters venturing into men's locker rooms was creating quite a stir. So I decided to demonstrate what would happen if a man made his way into a women's locker room. I needed an accomplice to pull off the story, and I found one in Ceal Barry, the University of Cincinnati women's basketball coach.

Ceal had played in the highly successful women's program at the University of Kentucky, and had landed the head coaching job at UC in her mid-twenties. This was her first year, and she was looking for ways to promote her program. She conspired with her players to help me with a rather daring stunt.

I took a cameraman to the entrance of the women's locker room, and began my TV report by saying, "Since women are now allowed to go into men's locker rooms, I don't see any reason why I shouldn't be able to visit the Lady Bearcats in theirs."

I opened the door, and walked in while the camera rolled. The players started screaming and throwing articles of clothing at me. I raised my hand and said, "Listen, I'm just here to talk about basketball. You've got a big game coming up this week..." and at that moment, two of the players came up from behind and doused me with a *huge* bucket of Gatorade. Hundreds of thousands of viewers heard the sound of liquid sucking into the microphone, and watched me shiver in shock as the icy cold drink soaked through my suit. In mock indignation, I looked into the camera and said, "This is the last time I'll ever report from inside a *women's* locker room!" I tossed the microphone on the floor and, dripping wet, stomped out.

Memorable sports coverage, folks. It certainly created a buzz for me at Channel 5, and for Ceal and her ascending hoops program.

Having found the courage to invade the UC women's locker room gave me the courage to ask Ceal out. I took her to an upscale pub/restaurant called "The 20 Mile House," so named because it was 20 miles from downtown. After dinner, we ordered the house specialty, Irish Coffee flamed tableside, then we advanced to the bar area and whooped it up to the tunes of a hot local band named Rainmaker. It was a beautiful, chaste, fun evening shared between a young television sportscaster and a rising college basketball coach. It felt nice.

I was growing in maturity, but soon found out that I had a long way to grow— spiritually and emotionally—regarding women. A TV exec introduced me to a gorgeous brunette whom I will call Morgan. She had the most beautiful, shimmering brown hair gently hanging to just above her waist. Her big brown eyes were mesmerizing. Each of her features seemed perfect from head-to-toe. I rarely had more than one night a week away from the late-night TV studio, but I began spending almost every free night with Morgan.

Morgan had grown up without a moral compass regarding sex, and she was always tempting me to break the 6th Commandment. At this point, of course, I knew, thanks to Corinthians and the Saginaw Franciscan, that unmarried sex was wrong. But Morgan didn't agree, and she tried to get me to see it her way.

Finding her temptations very hard to resist, I made the decision to stop seeing her. And I did it in a very abrupt way. I simply never called her again.

While I told myself I was being virtuous, I was really being selfish. Had I been truly mature, I would have called, and, if I was concerned for her soul, I would have found some way to tell her *why* I needed to cut things off. If I had integrity, I would have told her that she was meant for far more in a relationship, and that using each other for sexual pleasure was a cheap substitute. But instead, I simply ran.

TOO HOT TO HANDLE

Each spring, reporters from the area television stations went to Florida to cover the Cincinnati Reds in spring training. My competition was sending back the obligatory talking heads, so I decided to spice things up. I approached the Reds' future Hall of Fame catcher Johnny Bench, and told him I wanted to do a tongue-in-cheek story about what spring training is *really* all about. He gave me a smile and I could tell he was curious.

I said, "Here it is, Johnny. You and I go lie on recliners by a swimming a pool in our bathing suits, and talk about how *rigorous* spring training really is."

Johnny's smile grew wider and he said, "I'll tell you what, Zip. See those two girls outside the fence on their bikes? If you can get those girls to put on bikinis and meet us at the pool, I'll do it!"

I said, "You're on!"

I hurried over to the young ladies, and found that they were college students from Indiana. They were on spring break and had come down to watch their favorite players.

So I said, "Ladies, the great Johnny Bench has requested your appearance in a TV shoot this afternoon." Well, they all but swooned. "All you have to do is get in your bikinis, and meet us at the team hotel pool at 2 o'clock."

I almost flipped when one of them pulled up her t-shirt and said, "Look! We already have our bikinis on!" Sometimes in life, things go well beyond belief.

So at two o'clock, there we were—one of baseball's all-time greats, Johnny Bench, and yours truly lying side-by-side on recliners, poolside. To this day, I thank Bench for playing the role to the hilt. The feature opened with a shot of his famous face, his eyes shielded under his designer sunglasses. The camera shot pulled out to reveal us in perhaps the most relaxed position for a baseball interview in history. I began peppering Bench with presumably serious questions, like, "Johnny, I know there are a lot of big decisions you have to make during spring training, right?"

He'd respond in total deadpan with, "That's right Zip, *tough* decisions like, what kind of suntan lotion to use—or on some days—how many holes of golf to play." Of course, at one point, the college girls in bikinis walked in and presented us with cocktails, and we just shook our heads and moaned about how laborious it was to be in Florida for spring training.

That evening, I did the 6pm sportscast on location, and introduced the poolside interview. The piece caused such a stir that they repeated it on the 11pm news. A few days later, Bench approached me and asked, "Zip, how many times did they run that piece?"

I answered, "Twice."

He said, "They must have run it a lot more than that, because every friend I have has been calling me about the damn thing." It was a good thing for Johnny that YouTube hadn't been invented yet.

CATCH AND SHOOT

I've always thought the Harlem Globetrotters are among the most entertaining figures in sports. Over the decades, they have trotted to more than 100 countries to entertain fans young and old. I knew that when the Trotters came into a town, they often let a local celebrity or media personality make a token appearance as an honorary member of their famous foe, the Washington Generals. So when they came into Cincy, I made sure that I was *that* personality.

The Globetrotters have played the Generals something like 18,000 times, and they've hardly ever lost. This begs the question of whether Globetrotters games are fixed. As a keen observer of sports, I concluded that the answer is, "No." The reason the Globetrotters always win is because their players are bigger, stronger, faster and more talented than the players on the Generals. Thus, I was a natural General.

The Globetrotters hit the court on a weeknight at Riverfront Coliseum. I did the 6pm sportscast on Channel 5 and then hustled down to the Generals locker room. The team was made up of former college players of decent ability, who were accustomed to the intrusion of a media personality. The only instruction they gave me before the game was, "When the Globetrotters go into their famous weave near midcourt, don't try to be a hero and steal the ball, just follow the man you're guarding wherever he goes." I had no problem with that.

Soon after the game got underway, I made my appearance. It's tradition for the Globetrotters to let the local celebrity take a shot to entertain the fans. Most celebrities wind up missing, or hitting the side of the backboard or whatever. But remember, *the one thing I could do was shoot!*

One of the Generals passed me the ball along the baseline and I drilled a 15-footer. The crowd cheered. Naturally, the next time down the court, the Generals passed me the ball again, and I nailed a jumper from 18 feet. Louder cheers. The Globetrotters responded at the other end with a trick pass and a high-flying dunk. But, a couple minutes later, I again found myself open and bombed away from 20 feet. Perfect swish! The crowd was going wild. They had no idea I could actually *play basketball!* Personally, I was amazed I was keeping the Washington Generals in the game.

Uh, I must tell you that my sharp-shooting did not go unnoticed by the Trotters. I took a pass in the lane, and looked up to see one of their 7-foot superstars staring me in the face. As I looked up at the basket he said, "Go ahead, shoot!"

I hesitated. I thought, *this is a blocked shot waiting to happen.* But I didn't want to wimp out and pass the ball back out, so I aimed for the glass and banked the shot in. I was amazed that the 7-footer just stood there.

Then suddenly, the giant grabbed me by the shorts, and all the Globetrotters picked me up and carried me to their bench, and pretended like they were beating the hell out of me. Confetti was flying. The crowd roared with laughter. As the game continued, I managed to hit another jumper, and then late in the half, I found myself under the basket in the same kind of situation as before. Again, the 7-footer said, "Go ahead, shoot!" So I did. And he knocked the ball halfway up to the balcony. The Trotters always get the last laugh.

When the half ended, I went to the Generals locker room, changed into my suit, and headed back to the TV station. The Globetrotters rolled to an easy victory in the second half, but it didn't matter. On the late news, the sports fans of Cincinnati watched highlights of their little sports anchor scoring 10 points in the first half against the Harlem Globetrotters.

TAPPING OUT A TUNE

My TV career was going good. Too good. With my contract expiring, the station offered me a new three-year deal. But that's where pride kicked in. I didn't want to lock myself into Cincinnati for another three years when I felt I was good enough to move up and become rich and famous. So I worked without a contract for several months until the station basically said, "Sign the three-year deal, or take a hike!"

I put on my walking boots.

I agreed to do the sportscasts through the Christmas holidays, then depart. This was dicey. If I didn't find a job in a bigger market by Christmas, I'd have to find another way to make a living.

Meanwhile, the Cincinnati Bengals were having the greatest season in their history. I was at LaRosa's restaurant after a 6pm sportscast, chomping on a Kentucky Hot Brown when an inspiration popped into my mind: *write a song about the Bengals!* I wrote the first half of the lyrics over dinner, went back to the TV station, did the 11 o'clock sports, went home and finished the song at two in the morning.

The first stanza described how the legendary Paul Brown founded the Bengals as an NFL expansion team. The next verse celebrated the team's high-scoring offense, featuring the nicknames of the most popular players. The third verse was a tribute to the ferocious heroes of the Bengals' D. And the rousing chorus predicted that the Bengals would go on to win the Super Bowl!

There was one challenge left. I had no musical talent with which to record the song. Well, remember the 20-Mile House, and my date with Coach Ceal Barry? Remember the band, Rainmaker?

I tracked Rainmaker down, and told them I needed to cut a record. They jumped right in, creating a solid bass line, plus a little melody for the chorus. I'd be the main voice, and as I could not sing, I'd do it rap style. In 1981, no one had ever heard of rap.

We headed into a Cincinnati studio, a one-stop shop that recorded songs and pressed the vinyl right on the premises.

72

As a new client, I had to answer some pre-session questions.

"What's the name of your record label?"

My record label? "Um, uh—it's Championship Records!"

"What's your label design?"

"It's, uh—an image of the Bengals helmet!"

"What's the title of the song?"

"The title is—well, *of course*, the title is—'The Ballad of the Bengals'!"

We knocked out the song in about 4 hours. My adrenaline was flowing.

"Make me 15,000 copies."

I ran around to some radio stations, and they all started playing the song. The next challenge was distribution. In the music industry, the major record labels muscle their way into record stores, and the label and stores take most of the proceeds. So I cut out the middlemen. Mom-and-pop businesses and retailers who had *never sold records* put them on their shelves.

The biggest hit was at convenience stores. They put the records next to the register, so that anyone coming in to pay for gas, or buy gum, couldn't miss them! With Christmas approaching, "The Ballad" was a perfect gift.

The Bengals kept winning, and the record skyrocketed. I did interview after interview, and the stores ordered more and more.

The day before the Bengals' first-ever appearance in the AFC Championship Game, a popular FM radio station put me into their tricked out van, painted with orange and black Bengal stripes, to sell records with the "Bengal Brothers." We'd pull into a mall parking lot and the on-air DJ would say, "The Bengal Mobile is at Florence Mall!" Cars flooded the lot like it was Black Friday.

The temperature was three degrees above zero. I jumped out of the van and autographed records until my hand almost froze off. We sold hundreds of copies in about fifteen minutes. The Bengal Brothers collected the money as the crowd all but crushed us. We jumped back into the Bengal Mobile, and got the heck out of there before the authorities could arrest us for selling without a vendor's license.

When we were safely in the van, the on-air DJ would announce, "The Bengal Mobile is heading to our next secret location!"

We went to about five malls, and while we froze our asses, we were never apprehended. I can't remember how many records we sold, but it took a long time to count up and divide the money when we got back to the radio station.

Inviting everyone to fine dining in Cincinnati

In three weeks, we sold all 15,000 copies of the "The Ballad of the Bengals," making it the fastest-selling record in Cincinnati history. Unhappily, the Bengals lost the Super Bowl to Joe Montana and the 49ers, 21-16. I am certain that had the Bengals won, we could have pressed and sold another 50,000 copies.

As it was, I made enough money to support myself for five months. The problem was I would be out of work for longer than that.

WINDOW FINGERPRINTS

I put together tapes of my most colorful sportscasts, and sent them to N.S. Bienstock Inc., a giant in the TV agency field. They agreed to represent me. A personal agent named Steve promised he'd land me my next job in TV.

Filled with ego, I told Steve that I only wanted to work in one of six cities: New York, Washington, Boston, Philadelphia, Chicago, and my hometown of Detroit. That's right. The biggest cities in the East and the Midwest. Incredibly arrogant for an out-of-work 30-year-old sportscaster.

Weeks and months went by with no job offers. By the summer of 1982, I had gone through all the money I had made on the Bengals record, and was in dire need of cash. The Lord used the situation to teach me humility. Humility arrived in the form of a sales job.

Desperate for dough, I answered an ad for a replacement window salesman. I wasn't alone. At 9am on a Monday morning, I sat with 15 other unemployed people in a cramped, overcrowded office lobby. The owner appeared, scanned the crowd, and said, "Zip Rzeppa? *Zip Rzeppa???* Come with me."

His name was Marvin. He asked what the heck I was doing there. I told him I was waiting for my next job in TV and needed to make some money.

"Well, great! What do you know about selling windows?"

"Absolutely nothing." But a light went on in Marvin's head.

"No problem, you can work directly with me."

So every day I went with Marvin to visit people who needed their windows replaced. It seemed that in every home we entered, jaws dropped.

"Hey, aren't you…?"

Marvin would get their attention and tell them all about windows, and then they'd stare at me. I'd give them a big smile and say, "Look, I'm no expert on windows, but I know Marvin, and Marvin's a good, honest man, and I can attest to that!" Well, in those days, there were some shady window salesmen running around. No one wanted to get fleeced on replacement windows. My words were what the home-owners wanted to hear. Marvin and I closed deals at *every* home we visited! I had a heckuva future as a replacement window salesman.

HAND IT OVER

While I was hanging with Marvin, TV news guru Bill Applegate was hired to turn around Channel 7 in Boston, a station that had lingered in last place for years.

I jumped on the phone and called my agent Steve. My heart sank when he said, "Uhhhh, Zip, I really don't think you're Bill Applegate's kind of guy. I'm going on vacation and when I get back in a couple of weeks, I'll think about whether we want to send him a tape."

His reply ticked me off. So I whipped up a "Special Brief of the Qualifications of Zip Rzeppa for the Position of Sportscaster at WNEV-TV, Boston." I sent it to Applegate in a carton the size of a pizza box. The brief consisted of favorable newspaper articles about my success in Saginaw and Cincinnati, a tape of some of my most creative sportscasts, a free copy of "The Ballad of the Bengals" record, and an aggressive letter stating that I could help Applegate take Channel 7 from last place to first.

Almost immediately, my phone rang. Applegate told me to get on a plane to Boston. I aced the interview and he hired me on the spot. Overjoyed, I returned to Cincinnati, said goodbye to Marvin, and headed to Beantown.

On my first day at work in Boston, to my great surprise, I found myself shaking hands with my old college buddy, Bill O'Reilly.

"What are you doing here, Zip?"

"Hey, they just hired me to do the sports. What are *you* doing here, Bill?"

"Hey, they just hired me to do the news!" Hard to believe. Two guys who had met in 1974 at Boston University, who had traveled many a mile and worked at many a TV station in between, were suddenly working together at the big Channel 7 in Boston.

We each rented condos in Harbor Towers, the 40-story, I.M. Pei-designed twin skyscrapers on the waterfront. I was on the 37th floor with a balcony overlooking the harbor leading into the Atlantic Ocean. It was a pleasant, 10-minute walk to the TV station. Life was beautiful.

I was on the job for about three weeks when I got a call from my agent, Steve, in New York.

"Hey, I heard you got the job in Boston."

"That's right," I replied, anticipating what was coming.

"Congratulations. Uh, that's great. Soooo, if the contract isn't finalized, uh, we can take care of that for you."

I'm thinking, duh, right. Like, I'd go to work *without a contract*.

"The contract's done, Steve."

"Ahhhh. I see. Well, you know you have this agreement with us, and you owe us six percent."

"I owe you nothing, Steve. You were supposed to get me a job. I told you weeks ago that I wanted to work in Boston. You said, *'I don't think you're Bill Applegate's kind of guy.'* Remember?"

"Well, I guess I was wrong."

I grunted. "I guess so, too. I sent Applegate the tape, and he hired me. By the way, how was your vacation?"

He cleared his throat. "Uh, Zip, we still have this agreement. We are your representative."

"Steve, our agreement says you get 6% of any contract you negotiate for me. You negotiated nothing. 6% of nothing is nothing."

The truth is the truth. He said, "We'll get back to you on this."

I never heard from him again.

REACHING FOR A STAR

While O'Reilly and I teamed up to anchor the 6pm and 11pm newscasts on Saturdays and Sundays, my social interests focused on the weeknight anchor. Her name was Robin Young. She was the younger sister of the Hollywood actor, John Savage. She was cute and perky and fun. But I couldn't ask her out. One thing stood in the way. One of the great jazz musicians in the world. She was dating Pat Metheny.

I didn't want to horn in on their relationship or anything, but I was greatly attracted to Robin. I thought about what we had in common. In addition to TV, we were both runners. I found out she was going to run in a five-mile race on Thanksgiving Day. In my hyperactive imagination, I looked at the race as a possible chance for Robin and me to bond. But it was going to be a challenge. Co-workers told me she ran very fast. I always had a thing for fast women.

I trained and trained for weeks, and concocted my plan. The starting line was about a mile from my condo, so I'd stroll over, find Robin, chat, stretch with her, and get ready to run. Sound strategy.

But somehow, I *overslept*. In a panic, I left my condo and *ran* to the starting line, hoping that the race would be delayed a bit, and I could find Robin in the pack. It didn't happen. By the time I got to the start, the runners had taken off. I had already run a mile, so the five-mile race suddenly turned into a six-miler. I managed to catch and pass many of the walkers and slower runners, but I never caught sight of the speedy Robin. She probably was at home taking a shower by the time I hit the finish line.

That's pretty much how things went. Pat Metheny turned out to be a nice guy. He loved the Celtics and the way I covered the team. He took off on a European tour, and Robin remained ultra-loyal to him, so I was left looking for love elsewhere.

STICKY FINGERS

Soon after I arrived in Boston, a circuit court judge ruled that a girl had the right to play on a high school *football* team. In the culture of the day, the case was about women's rights. A few days later, when a local high school boy was granted permission to play on the girls' field hockey team, I smelled a story.

The boy's name was Arnold. Questions swirled in my head. Was he doing this to spite the girl who got to play on the boys' football team? Did he truly *love* field hockey so much he just *had* to be on the team? Was he simply looking for a clever way to hang with girls?

In search of answers, I took a camera crew out to meet Arnold. The field hockey team, known as the Lady Bears, was playing an afternoon game. We arrived a few minutes after the action started. Out on the grass, there was Arnold, running around and competing with and against the girls. Like his teammates, he was wearing a little plaid skirt and knee socks.

Before long, Arnold scored a goal. His teammates treated him as one of their own. They gathered around him and whooped and hollered, raising their sticks in the air. The Lady Bears went on to win 6-2. Clearly, they would have won with or without Arnold.

Immediately after the game, I hustled onto the field with the film crew. Somehow, Arnold wasn't surprised that he was the player I wanted to interview.

I opened with, "Congratulations on the win, Arnold. You guys— uh, you girls—uh, your *team*—played really well today."

He answered like a seasoned pro. "I want to give the other team credit. They played hard, but everything seemed to be clicking for us today. It was a lot of fun."

After he answered a couple of other routine questions, I cleared my throat and said, "You know, for some reason, Arnold, I never *personally* had a desire to *play* field hockey when I was your age. If I put this microphone down, could you show me some of the finer points of the game?"

He nodded, so I dropped the microphone and someone handed me a field hockey stick. The camera captured us squaring off, eyeball to eyeball, in a head-and-shoulders shot. As the ball was dropped and we began to skirmish, the camera panned out to reveal that below my blazer and shirt and tie, I, too, was wearing a little field hockey skirt. Hilarious.

FIST BUMP

One of my joys was covering Larry Bird and his mighty Boston Celtics. This was the 1980s, the period of Larry's great rivalry with Magic Johnson and the Lakers.

I had known Magic since he was in high school. While working in Saginaw, I covered him as he led Lansing Everett High to an overtime victory in the Michigan state championship game against my alma mater, the good ol' Brother Rice Warriors.

I was at the press conference when he announced his college choice. It came down to Big Ten power Michigan and struggling Michigan State. With the cameras rolling, Magic said, "Michigan *wants* me—but Michigan State *needs* me. I'm gonna be a Spartan."

Two years later, I risked my life on the icy Michigan highways between Saginaw and East Lansing to shoot highlights of his *magical* season as he led the Spartans to the national championship over Bird and Indiana State. Their 1979 NCAA title matchup remains the most watched college game of all time.

Magic was in his fourth season in the NBA when he came into Boston with the Lakers. After the morning shoot-around, I dropped by the locker room. Magic's first name was Earvin, but everybody called him by his colorful nickname. I decided to greet him by his *other* nickname, the one used only by his family and close friends back home.

"Hey, EJ—how you doing?"

He immediately threw me his familiar, infectious grin. "Home boy! What are you doin' here?" He didn't remember my name, but his friendly *home boy* touched me.

"I'm working here at Channel 7."

He chuckled. "Man, you're covering the wrong team."

It was my turn to laugh. The Magic Man gave me a sincere one-on-one interview, with heartfelt responses instead of the tired clichés. Great TV.

THE FICKLE FINGER OF FATE

On and off the air, O'Reilly and I were having plenty of fun. One night we were lured into a comedy club by the proprietor, a comic named Mike McDonald. Mike said, "You gotta come and see this new guy. He's tremendous!" O'Reilly and I yawned through the warm-up acts until McDonald's star came out. And the guy wowed us. Laugh-out-loud funny. He did it without any off-color humor, which was rare. Obviously, he was working hard at his craft.

McDonald brought the comedian over to join us at our table. I wondered if a comic with a chiseled jaw and a New England accent could make it outside of Boston. Well, as it turned out, he persisted, and he did okay. He made more than a *quarter of a billion dollars* as the host of *The Tonight Show,* and he frequently invited O'Reilly to be his celebrity guest.

But that night, I was just having fun with my buddy, O'Reilly, and this guy, Jay Leno.

Back at work, the Channel 7 weekend newscasts were a blast. Going into commercial breaks, O'Reilly would say stuff like, "Coming up next, the man Larry Bird loves to party with, the 'Big Z,' Zip Rzeppa, with sports!" I never partied with Larry, but it certainly left the viewers wondering.

Things really got crazy on the set on Super Bowl weekend in 1982. On the eve of the big game, I predicted in no uncertain terms that Dan Marino and the Miami Dolphins would defeat the Washington Redskins. The next evening, John Riggins and the Redskins clobbered the Dolphins. So I had to own up to my prediction-gone-awry on the 11pm sportscast.

Naturally, O'Reilly opened with, "So—what happened to that prediction of yours?"

I responded, "I know, Bill, I know. Kinda got it wrong. Boy, do I have egg on my face." At which point, I took a raw egg and smashed it on my forehead. Chaos ensued. The woman co-anchor started shrieking, the cameramen were on the floor laughing, and O'Reilly was throwing me a towel.

As the yolk dripped down my face, I proceeded to roll through the highlights of how the Dolphins did *not* win the Super Bowl. O'Reilly cracked, "That was great, but what are you gonna eat for breakfast?" There was a buzz around the newsroom after the show.

I was thinking, *well, just another colorful sportscast!* I was totally unprepared for the commotion that ensued. The station was deluged with calls and letters from viewers both for and against the stunt. A big problem was the reaction of Boston's two daily newspapers. The Boston Globe called me "unprofessional." I thought the colorful tabloid, The Boston Herald, would have enjoyed the humor, but their TV critic clobbered me even harder. To make matters worse, he wouldn't let it go. Whenever he mentioned me in a story thereafter, he *always* referred to me as "Zip Rzeppa, the man who smashed an egg on his face." I had to tell him that was not part of my name.

A few days later, the station general manager called me into his office. Unhappily, he was in the camp of those who saw *the egg act* as going too far. Years later, the esteemed University of Missouri School of Journalism began showing the egg tape to aspiring broadcast students, asking, "What do you think of that? Good? Bad? Clever? Outrageous?" I've been told there's been plenty of debate.

*The Channel 7 news team in Boston, me and O'Reilly on the left,
when we had much more hair.*

HEAVY HANDED

A few months after the egg smashing incident, the wheels were coming off at Channel 7. Applegate's strategy to turn the station around wasn't working. The so-called Silver Fox got out-of-town ahead of the pack.

He was replaced by a man I will call Mr. Clean. Early 30s, full head of carefully coiffed blonde hair, nice suits. He had a strong preference for straight-forward newscasts. In other words, he didn't like colorful. You can guess who his two least favorite anchors were.

But before he dealt with O'Reilly and me, he fired our friend, weekend weathercaster, Shane Hollett, and replaced him with Art Horn. Art was a nice enough young guy, but on the air he was meek and mild, totally nondescript. Of course, O'Reilly didn't want any of that on his newscast, so he nicknamed Horn, 'The Hammer.' At the end of a weathercast, O'Reilly would bellow things like, "Hey, if 'The Hammer' says it's gonna storm, you better *run for cover!*" Then he would swing over to me to preview the sports and it was all I could do to keep from cracking up.

Mr. Clean went on to wipe away reporters like spots on the floor. I was among them.

I had gone out-of-town on my regular days off, and when I returned to Boston, a stranger walked up to me and said, "I'm so sorry."

I looked at him, confused. "Sorry about what?"

"About you getting fired!"

"Fired?" I gulped. "You mean, *me?* What are you talking about?"

He shook his head. "It's been in the papers for two days."

It wasn't a lot of fun to be fired in the newspapers.

Our bright, bubbly, fun, and edgy newscast had been flushed down the toilet. In my seven years in TV, I'd seen quite a few people get fired, but I never believed it would happen to me. I had to face some harsh realities: saying goodbye to the job I loved, looking for work in another city, and knowing that O'Reilly and I would be going in different directions. I was unemployed.

Seeing me in a vulnerable place, the Evil One went on the attack.

I started going to daily Mass at St. Anthony's Shrine, a short walk from my condo. To get there, I had to pass an adult bookstore which kept its outside doors wide open, and offered scores of pornographic magazines for 50 cents. Satan spoke to my heart. "You're out of work, but at 50 cents, you can buy these every day. They'll make you feel better." The temptation was relentless.

Jesus Christ, the Light of the World, was present in the Blessed Sacrament at the Shrine. Right next door, in typical flashy fashion, the forces of evil invited me to seek pleasure in empty lust. The battle of Good vs. Evil. In my weakness, I wanted to buy those magazines, but I feared that God wasn't going to help me find a job if I allowed porn to take hold of me.

Through the grace of God, I *always* walked past the temptation.

SWEATY PALMS

I hired Art Kaminsky to be my agent. Art represented count-less local and network TV personalities, plus dozens of professional athletes. He loved my colorful style.

He sent a tape of some of my most creative sportscasts to Cliff Abromats, who had just landed the job of news director at the number one station in the number one market in the country, WABC-TV, Channel 7, in New York. Art hardly needed to. Cliff had seen me in action on a daily basis when he managed a competing station in Cincinnati.

WABC-TV was tops in news coverage, but two giants working for competing stations, Marv Albert and Warner Wolf, dominated New York's sports coverage. Cliff thought I just might be the guy to take them on.

My mind flashed back to all those Greyhound bus rides as I *flew* to New York for the biggest interview of my life. Walking toward Cliff's office through the electric atmosphere of the nation's top local TV newsroom, I felt exhilarated and slightly intimidated at the same time.

The interview started well. I could envision myself sitting in the big anchor chair. Then Abromats threw three booklets on the table in front of me. He finger-pointed me and said, "I want you to memorize every word here. These are the union rules and regulations. If I hire you, there will be union personnel who will do everything they can to *cut your throat* and see that you fail. You *must* know *everything* that they can and cannot do to you."

I didn't know what to say. I was the fun-loving sportscaster who made everyone laugh. Why would people want to destroy me? I looked at Cliff and mumbled, "Okay, uhhh, I'll take a look at these booklets."

I truly believe that in that response, Abromats decided I wasn't tough enough for the position. Had I responded, "Listen pal, I played quarterback on one of the roughest, toughest high school teams in Detroit. I played basketball in the ghettos as the only white guy on the court. I'm not afraid of nothin' or nobody," then I really think I would have gotten the job. As it turned out, I never got to the sit in the anchor chair at Channel 7. Instead, I wound up back on the couch in my condo in Boston.

As autumn turned to winter, a cloud covered my mind and a storm raged in my spirit. How could I reach my dream job in Boston and then lose it because a new boss didn't appreciate creativity? How could I get so close to the mega job in New York, and not get it? If I was that close, I had to be one of the best in America, right? No way would I pursue a job in a small market. Still unemployed, I wouldn't settle for anything less than the big time.

Weeks and months went by. I was rapidly running out of money. I began to wonder if Marvin the Window Salesman had a branch office in Boston.

In the darkness of the New England winter, I seldom left my condo. I had slipped into depression when O'Reilly came to my aid. He knocked on my door, came in, and shook me up. He yelled, "Hey, you're depressed, you gotta get out of here! You're sittin' around all day, doin' nothing!"

I feebly replied, "No, Bill, I'll be okay, I'm gonna get back in the game soon."

Bill dragged me out to a movie that night, and he never stopped encouraging me to get up and get going, to climb out of my depressed state. His friendship at that critical time is something for which I cannot adequately express my gratitude.

After parting ways with Mr. Clean, O'Reilly began hosting a new one-hour show, "New England Afternoon." The program was short-lived, and Bill joined me in the land of the unemployed. He wasn't out of work for long. Showing greater humility than me, he accepted a news anchor job in Portland, Oregon, the 38th biggest market.

ON THE OTHER HAND

I'd been out of work for five long months when Art Kaminsky told me a station in St. Louis had an interest. It was KTVI-TV, Channel 2, at that time, the ABC-TV affiliate. The situation was the reverse of Boston. Their current sports guy had a straightforward style. They were looking for someone colorful. *Colorful* was my middle name.

They didn't want their sports guy to know he was about to get fired, so they flew me from Boston to their sister station in Syracuse to do an audition. On a snowy, winter afternoon, I researched, wrote, and produced a sportscast, and then performed it on tape. Through the grace of God, there wasn't any rust. I nailed it. They sent the tape to St. Louis.

Channel 2 took a look and immediately offered me a two-year contract to do their 5pm, 6pm, and 10pm Monday-through-Friday sportscasts.

The only problem was, St. Louis was not my dream. I only wanted to work in New York, Chicago, Philadelphia, Boston, Washington, or my home town of Detroit. With my pride running amok, I turned down the offer.

Channel 2 didn't like my answer. They flew me to St. Louis. They told me they *really* wanted me, and dramatically increased their offer. I told them I'd think about it. I flew back to Boston.

At this point, my agent, Art, and my dear mother in Detroit, started going ballistic. They were yelling, "You've been out of work for five months! Take the job!"

Incredibly, I continued to resist. I went to New York to meet with Alfred Geller. Geller had a reputation for putting together some of the most lucrative deals in all of television. His clients only worked in the biggest cities.

I'll never forget walking into his office. It was a huge rectangular room, maybe 90 feet by 50 feet. The walls were covered with exquisite art. The only piece of furniture was this large desk, smack dab in the middle of the room, with Alfred sitting behind it. He motioned for me to walk over and have a seat.

He was a pudgy man, balding in front, with hair down to his shoulders in the back. Unlike most agents of the time, he did not bother to wear a tie. He was well aware of what had happened to me in Boston. I told him about the pending offer in St. Louis, and my hopes and dreams to work in one of the biggest cities in the country.

He looked at me and said with all certainty, "Well, you have a choice to make. If you go to St. Louis, you will be there forever."

I cut him off, and said, "No, if I go to St. Louis, I'll use it as a stepping stone to get back to a bigger city."

He looked back at me and said, "No, if you go to St. Louis, you will be so big, and they will love you so much, they will never let you leave, and you will never want to." He continued, saying, "Your other choice is to turn them down and hope against hope for a job in one of the biggest cities in America. You're good enough, but those jobs are few and far between, and it's possible you may never get the opportunity. The choice is yours."

I returned home to Boston. Throughout my life, I always enjoyed the freedom of deciding what I would do, where I would go, how I would live. But at this point, I was emotional toast. My decision would affect me for a long time, if not for the rest of my life. I was paralyzed by fear, terrified that I would make the *wrong* decision.

As a last resort, I got on my knees in front of the big window of my rented luxury condo on the 37th floor, overlooking the night lights of Boston, and for the first time in my life, I told God that I wanted to do His Will, not mine.

I let out a long, slow, deep breath. Instantly, all the anxiety and tension and uncertainty were gone. An incredible peace came over me, and I was certain of God's Will.

I left the sixth biggest market in the country, Boston, to move to the 18th biggest market, St. Louis.

WARM HANDSHAKES

I arrived in St. Louis on a Sunday night, exhausted from the 1,200 mile drive. Channel 2 bought me a room at the Howard Johnson's Motor Lodge, right off Highway 44. No limit to luxury! I flipped on the TV to scout my competition. I almost had a heart attack.

The sportscasters in St. Louis were competent professionals, but decidedly conservative and low-key. My style was fast-paced, packed with video, full of humor and hard hitting commentary. These Midwest folks weren't accustomed to that. If they didn't like it, I could see my next job being in, say, Alaska?

I wasn't about to change. I wouldn't smash an egg on my face, but I had absolutely no interest in doing bland, colorless sports reports. Zip had to be Zip, and I let it rip.

I launched a segment called, *The Zippo Awards*, for "the best, the worst, and the weirdest performances in the wild and wacky, wonderful world of sports." Picture *America's Funniest Home Videos* meets YouTube, only years before either existed. Soon, little kids were begging their parents to let them stay up and watch *The Zippos* at 10pm every Friday.

I took a call from a viewer named Steve Rupp.

"Welcome to town, Zip! Love your crazy sportscasts! You might like to know, we just created a new sport. It combines the two most *boring* sports to watch on TV: bowling and the luge."

Intrigued, I grabbed a camera crew and headed out to the snow-covered slope of Art Hill in Forest Park. Steve and two of his friends were catapulting down the hill on saucers, attempting to knock over bowling pins they set up at the bottom. The buddies wore ski masks. One was a partner in a law firm, the other a U.S. Prosecuting Attorney. The masks hid their identities from a public that may not understand the appeal of luge bowling.

When I showed the new sport on my 6pm sportscast, phones started ringing off the hook. The viewers loved it! The Midwest was ready for some extra zip in their sports!

Steve and his fellow luge bowlers invited me to a monthly lunch gathering called "First Fridays"—40 men in the basement of Del Pietro's Restaurant, all of them sports nuts. They gave me a standing ovation. For the next 90 minutes we yelled and screamed about the Cardinals, the Blues, the Olympics, everything. I felt the fun and passion, and couldn't wait for the next First Friday.

HAND TO MOUTH

The St. Louis Blues made a trade that brought Ricky Meagher back into my life. During our BU days, the undersized Meagher seemed a long shot to make it in the NHL. And with no money, no contacts, and a face made for radio, few would have predicted that *I'd* succeed in TV. Ten years later, we had beaten the odds. And what were the odds we'd *both* end up in St. Louis?

I headed to the Blues' locker room to greet the former Terrier.

"Ricky, welcome to town. Way back when, did you ever think we'd make it?"

He grinned. "Well, Zip, at least *I* could skate."

"Yeah, Rick, well, at least *I* could talk."

He asked if I had any hockey hijinks coming up, and I wasn't about to let him down. The next night, when the Blues were playing an inferior opponent, I promised the viewers, "If the Blues lose this game, I'll eat a hockey puck."

Most of St. Louis tuned in after the Blues lost. I had to make good on my pledge. I held up a hockey puck, and gave the anchors a wry grin. "I'll get to this!" After running through the Blues lowlights, I apprehensively, slowly moved the puck into my mouth, secretly slipping in a few white Chiclets. I grimaced, removed the puck, and spit out the Chiclets. To all the world, it looked like I was spitting out my teeth. The anchors cracked up. Half of St. Louis probably thought I was toothless, but at least I didn't have egg on my face.

Things were cooking. Channel 2 even turned my looks into an advantage. They produced a promotional spot highlighting my zany antics, and capped it with the tagline: "Zip Rzeppa—More Than Just *Another* Pretty Face!"

I whipped up colorful coverage of the Cardinals. As the "Runnin' Redbirds" raced to three World Series appearances in the '80s, my exuberant commentary helped me run away with the ratings. The other stations were forced to change philosophy—and personnel—in an effort to compete.

HANDS OFF

Along the way, I had a rift with the Cardinals future Hall of Fame manager, Whitey Herzog. A long rift.

In the dual role of Manager/GM, Herzog had acquired Ozzie Smith, Willie McGee, and others in a series of shrewd trades, and guided the Cards to the World Series title in 1982. But by spring training 1985, storm clouds appeared. The team failed to contend in '83 and '84, and then lost Hall of Fame reliever Bruce Sutter to free agency. Whitey's champion, team owner Gussie Busch, turned 86 and was stepping down. Lawyers were taking over. They hired Tal Smith as a consultant.

When Tal was an executive with the Yankees, they hired Bill Virdon as manager. When he took over the front office of the Astros, he brought in Virdon to manage. So when I arrived at spring training '85 and found Virdon in uniform as a "special instructor," I thought, uh-oh. If the Cards falter, Tal Smith might be replacing Whitey with Virdon.

I filed a report from Florida, informing the viewers of this possible scenario. I loved Whitey, so I wanted the fans to know that behind the scenes, danger lurked. Whitey never saw my report, but some of his friends saw it and called him, and he misinterpreted the message.

A month later, I traveled to New York to cover the team's season opener. The Cardinals suffered a very tough loss, and Whitey was understandably ticked off. When I walked in to interview him, he went off on me, right in front of numerous members of the media.

"Zip, I'm not talking to you. You're trying to get me fired."

I was confused. "Huh? What?"

"You did that story from Florida. You said Bill Virdon's going to replace me. Bill's a friend of mine. You're trying to get me fired."

"Whitey, I never said…no, Whitey. No, I was trying to help you, to let people know that behind the scenes—"

He cut me off. "You're trying to get me fired!" Then he shouted, "I'll never talk to you again."

And for the Cardinals entire pennant-winning season of 1985, he never talked to me.

In the relaxed atmosphere of the following spring training, I approached the Cardinals skipper.

"Whitey, I'm sorry we had a misunderstanding last year. I was in no way trying to get you fired. I—"

"Zip, I don't care. I don't want to hear it. I'm still not talking to you." Another season, no interviews with Whitey.

The following spring, 1987, I asked Bob Costas to intercede for me. Bob had been a witness to Whitey's blow-up in New York, and he said he'd smooth things over. He returned wearing a frown.

"Zip, I don't know what you said in that report, but he's still mad. He's not going to talk to you." Another season went by.

Spring training, 1988. I asked the Cardinals Hall of Fame radio broadcaster, Jack Buck, who was always very kind to me, to approach Whitey. Jack said he'd be glad to, that he'd find a way to bring us together. Same result. Jack was baffled. "I don't get it, kid, but he's not going to talk to you."

I couldn't figure it out. Whitey managed the Cardinals to the World Series in both 1985 and 1987, so maybe he was thinking, *let's not change things.*

Spring training, 1989. I implored the Cardinals vice-president of communications, Jeff Wehling, to bring about a reconciliation. "I'm aware of this rift, Zip. We'll get it straightened out."

Again, failure. Another season, no interviews with Whitey.

In spring training of 1990, I decided to make the annual pitch to Whitey myself. I figured it was futile, but I'd take a shot. To my surprise, he didn't blow me off. "Zip, how long has it been since I did an interview with you?"

"Five years."

"Well, Zip, I think you've paid your dues. We can talk again."

I was overjoyed. The five-year rift was over! I did a long, one-on-one interview with Whitey—the greatest interview I ever did! Whitey gave me the scoop about how he and Gussie Busch used to meet at the old man's country place, and drink beer and eat blood sausage, and how he convinced Gussie that all the trades he wanted to make were the right ones, and how he built the Cards into the team that made it to three World Series in six years. He told colorful story after story about the glory days.

I turned the interview into a 10-part series during the spring TV ratings period, and we absolutely blew away the competition.

Less than two months later, Whitey surprised the ballclub, his players, the fans, and the city by resigning as Cardinals manager in the middle of the season. A million thoughts were going through my head.

Was Whitey thinking about quitting when he reconciled with me? He knew I'd put all those colorful stories on TV. It would give the fans something to remember. Or did he do the interview to keep me from saying anything bad? Deep down, I like to think Whitey respected me, and he simply forgave me for any offense.

Through the years, we've seen each other at a few events, and we've had pleasant chats. All is well. For me, it was a great pleasure to cover the fabulous Cardinals teams managed by one of the greatest baseball managers of all time. It was well worth the Silent Treatment.

HANDS FULL

In 1986, my parish, Our Lady of Lourdes, offered the *Renew* program, a series of small-group gatherings to discuss and apply Scripture to daily life. Because of my wacky TV hours, I circled "weekday mornings" as my available time frame.

Thus, I was placed in a group with five middle-aged women. Them and me. If the mix wasn't *uncomfortable enough* for a 34-year-old male, what made it really *awkward* was that the woman hosting the gatherings was Nancy Bidwill. Her husband, Bill, owned the St. Louis Cardinals NFL team.

It was my job to report on his team, which was no easy task, as his Cardinals had muddled through poor drafts and poorer performances on the field, and were threatening to leave St. Louis and move to Arizona. Hello, Nancy, nice coming into your home to pray with you!

During the six weeks of *Renew,* we never mentioned her husband's NFL team. We kept it to Scripture and daily life, but even that was weird. I was young, single, male, a TV sportscaster. They were all middle-aged, married, female, mothers. You think anyone felt like really *opening up*?

Anyway, it was a good thing we never mentioned the football team, because I was doing the radio color commentary of the Cardinals games, and true to my style, I wasn't holding back about the ineptitude of the franchise as it struggled through another losing season. My honest commentary so irritated Mr. Bidwill that at mid-season, he asked the radio station to add a team-friendly analyst to the booth, to sugar-coat things. I threatened to quit if the station placated Bidwill, and to the station's credit, they did *not* add another commentator.

In the midst of it all, Bidwill was demanding that St. Louis build him a new stadium. City officials balked. In response, Bidwill was flying to Phoenix, a city hungry for an NFL team, to meet with courtiers from the desert.

I decided to crash the negotiations.

It was 18 below zero when I got in a cab and headed to the airport. It was sunny and 72 when I arrived in Phoenix. I got a tip that Bidwill would be attending a Super Bowl party at the home of a big wig who was trying to woo him west. The party host and his guests were surprised to see an uninvited guy from St. Louis and his sidekick stroll in. At least my videographer left the TV gear in the rental.

Bidwill was even more shocked to see me, but it was surprisingly easy for me to entice him to do the interview. We set up on the deck of this multi-million dollar home in the desert, and I peppered him with questions about his intentions. In retrospect, Bidwill was using me to deliver a message to the St. Louis city fathers that he was serious about moving. I didn't mind being the messenger.

A few months later, Bidwill moved the Cardinals to Arizona.

Riding high on the airwaves of St. Louis

HANDLE WITH CARE

By the end of my fourth year on St. Louis TV, my Q rating was reported to be the highest of all the local TV sportscasters in America. The Q referred to a broadcaster's familiarity plus popularity with viewers.

With my contract expiring, my good old agent, Art Kaminsky, told me he could get me a job almost anywhere. Four years earlier, I never would have dreamed of my response: "Art, I want to stay in St. Louis." Alfred Geller was right.

Art set up a bidding war among the top three St. Louis TV stations. All of them agreed to offer a five-year, guaranteed contract for 1.5 million dollars. In 1988, that was a whole lot of money.

Channel 2's news anchor had just jumped ship, so I got a brilliant idea. I told Channel 2 I'd stay with them if they'd hire Bill O'Reilly to anchor the news. Bill had escaped Portland, was back in Boston, but was relegated to doing short commentaries. He wanted to return to the anchor chair, and was willing to come to St. Louis. I was severely disappointed at Channel 2's response. "Bill O'Reilly? We think Bill is too controversial."

So I signed a 5-year contract to move to Channel 4.

Unhappily, there was a sticking point. I had a non-compete clause in my Channel 2 contract, which prohibited me from working at another TV station for six months. The good news was, my Channel 4 contract provided that I'd be paid in full whether I was on the air or not.

So I took advantage of the six months away from TV to concentrate on romance. I met a stunningly beautiful woman at a downtown party. Let's call her Alexis. She was a linguist, with a wonderful heart for the poor. She spoke fluent French and Spanish, and taught herself two tribal languages while working with the suffering in central Africa.

We hit it off right way. She had only a cursory knowledge of sports—and I could only speak one language—but we became close.

Then Alexis began exhibiting extreme behaviors.

We were in a rental car in a parking lot after attending the NCAA regional basketball tournament in North Carolina. I'll never know what triggered it. Alexis began pounding on the dash board and then physically attacking me. Sitting behind the wheel, it was difficult for me to defend myself and restrain her.

When we got back to St. Louis, I went with Alexis to see her therapist. I was aware that Alexis was the daughter of two alcoholic parents, but it took the therapist to explain the resultant devastating effect.

The therapist did not believe Alexis's condition could be cured. She told me any long-term relationship would be extremely difficult. I was dumbfounded. I didn't want to accept it. I couldn't believe that other people's drinking could have such a powerful effect on someone who did not drink herself.

A few weeks later, Alexis and I were sitting on my deck on a pleasant afternoon. I happened to mention that an anchorwoman I formerly worked with always looked very nice on-camera. As soon as I said this, Alexis got up and ran *right through the glass door* that led from the deck into my house, shattering it into a million pieces. She ran out the front door and down the street. In horror, I raced after her, and tackled her, at which point she started throwing punches. As she flailed away at the shadows of her past, I absorbed the blows.

Alexis had so much of what I was looking for. Brainy, beautiful, generous, and virtuously romantic. In spite of the alarming incidents, I didn't want to give up on her.

Then she called and said she was contemplating suicide.

I gently talked to her and she calmed down. Sadly, over the next couple of months, the calls continued.

I had to deal with reality. I had signed a contract to work until midnight for the next five years of my life. Alexis needed a guy who would be at home with her. I had to break things off.

I dearly wanted the best for Alexis, but I knew I wasn't the man for the job.

HANDS OF DESPAIR

When my six-month non-compete clause expired, I charged back into the nightly battle for St. Louis' TV sports viewers. But the landscape had changed. During my hiatus, our chief rival, Channel 5, crafted a series of promotional spots that garnered national attention. The spots were called, "Bob and Mike," and featured weathercaster, Bob Richards, and my direct competition, sportscaster Mike Bush. There they were, Bob and Mike, on the air, off the air, goofing around, doing all kinds of amusing things. People loved it. Fresh versions were continually produced. For many years, Bob and Mike provided formidable competition for us.

Until Bob committed suicide.

Bob was 38-years-old, making about $250,000 per year. He had a wife and an 11-year-old daughter, and a new home in the suburbs. Life *seemed* great. But Bob had a mistress. When the mistress cut off their relationship, Bob began stalking her. She went to court to get a restraining order.

The Associated Press, the St. Louis Post-Dispatch, and four St.

Louis television stations ran stories about the court case. The mistress went on a popular morning radio show. Other women called in, claiming Bob also had affairs with *them*.

The next night, after predicting mild and sunny weather on Channel 5's 10pm newscast, Bob went to Spirit of St. Louis airport. He flew his Red Piper Cherokee plane up to 400 feet, pointed the nose of the plane downward, and accelerated in a power dive. He died on impact.

St. Louis was in shock. In the glamourous world of TV, the Evil One can provide relentless temptations to serious sin, but it was horrific to see Bob Richards' life end in suicide.

WILD APPLAUSE

Shortly after I returned to the airwaves, the 1988 Summer Olympic Games took place in Seoul, South Korea. St. Louis rejoiced as one of its own, Jackie Joyner-Kersee, won two gold medals in spectacular fashion. Her score of 7,291 points in the heptathlon, a combination of seven track-and-field events, set a world record that still stands today. Everyone was celebrating Jackie. When she returned home, I clobbered the competition by getting her to do an exclusive 30-minute TV special.

Jackie took me and our videographer to the little house where she grew up in extreme poverty. She told me of the agony of watching her mother die from meningitis at the age of 37, and about her own continuing battle with asthma. She showed me how she and her young friends used to fill empty potato chip bags with sand to create a makeshift long jump pit. Very touching. We featured her husband,

Bob Kersee, whom she had met when he coached her at UCLA. We closed the program with Jackie talking about her dream of helping impoverished young people. Terrific TV.

Jackie fulfilled her dream by establishing the sprawling Jackie Joyner-Kersee recreation center in East St. Louis. Years later, I cried tears of joy when Sports Illustrated named Jackie the world's greatest female athlete of the 20th century.

HANDING IT OUT

I mentioned Jack Buck was among those who tried to help me with Whitey. Jack was one of the greatest radio announcers of all-time. He was inducted into the media wing of the Baseball Hall of Fame at Cooperstown in 1987. Countless millions heard his Cardinals broadcasts over 45 years, but far fewer got to see him emcee a banquet. He was the best I've ever seen. Jack would open with hilarious takes on current events, and then deliver witty, clever, pertinent remarks about half the people in the room. Many left quoting his lines, but *my* most memorable Jack Buck comment wasn't a joke.

Jack and I were sitting alone in the Cardinals media room when he told me that when he gets to Heaven, the first question he will ask the Lord is, *"Why were You so good to me?"*

Others no doubt have asked the same question about Jack. A number of people told me that on Cardinals road trips, Jack would surprise cab drivers, bellhops, and waiters by tipping them with a crisp $100 bill. Or two. Or three.

HANDLED LIKE A PRO

In 1990, Jack told me that his son, Joe, had his heart set on becoming a radio sports announcer. Jack had another idea. "I keep tellin' him, Zip, TV is where it's at!" Joe had just finished his junior year at Indiana University, so we gave him an unpaid summer internship at Channel 4.

Joe clearly had his sights set on the microphone. He was bored with the menial tasks of an intern, so I surprised him by assigning him to do a live interview with a major league player from Busch Stadium on my 6pm sportscast.

Joe was a bit nervous, but he was far more excited. For a moment, I had a flashback to Fort Wayne and my own nervousness and excitement before my first TV sportscast. As I tossed the show to Joe, I held my breath. In live TV, anything can happen. There was nothing to worry about! Joe showed exceptional confidence and poise in his first-ever TV appearance.

Seeing that he could handle it, we let Joe do a couple more live interviews before the summer ended. He never returned to Channel 4—and never graduated from Indiana University. He finished his education in the Cardinals radio booth, announcing games with his dad. At age 25, he became the NFL's youngest-ever regular TV play-by-play man. At age 27, he did the TV play-by-play of the World Series. He's done more World Series games than anyone in history, plus the TV play-by-play of four Super Bowls. Joe made his dad a prophet. "TV is where it's at!"

STICK HANDLING

Introducing NHL Hall of Famer Bernie Federko to the broadcasting world presented a different challenge. Bernie played exactly

1,000 games in his 14-year career, but he never won the Stanley Cup. His teams never even made it to the Finals.

Late in his career, coinciding with the St. Louis Blues annual elimination from the playoffs, I asked Bernie to make the transition from skates, sticks, and stitches to the world of suits, make-up, and live TV. We ran promos for "Sunday Nights with Bernie" to get all the depressed Blues fans to tune in.

It was sad for Bernie to talk about other players going after the Cup that he never won. It was sad for me just sitting next to him. But Bernie threw himself into the job with great intensity, and what he lacked in experience he made up for in enthusiasm.

Bernie is one of the nicest athletes I ever met, and I'm delighted he went on to become a big-time color commentator and analyst on the Blues' TV broadcasts.

WEARING GOLD GLOVES

My favorite major league baseball player, next to my childhood hero, Al Kaline, was Ozzie Smith. The Wizard of Oz won thirteen consecutive Gold Gloves as arguably the greatest fielding shortstop of all-time. I remember his dramatic walk-off home run in Game 5 of the 1985 NLCS against the Dodgers, the first homer he ever hit left-handed, as if it were yesterday.

Few knew how hard Ozzie worked. He had extremely quick hands and feet, and those assets alone would have made him terrific. But I saw him many times, out in the hot sun, hours before batting practice, fielding scorching ground balls. He designed drills to see how quickly he could move his hands as he snagged hundreds of grounders in practice every week.

He was *not* a natural hitter. He hit .231 over his first four major league seasons, but he worked his butt off to improve, and in 1987, when he finished second in the MVP voting, he hit .303.

I loved Oz as a player, and that love almost got me fired. After the death of Gussie Busch, Anheuser-Busch's lawyers were in charge. They let Ozzie become a free agent, and he began shopping his talents. I did a fist-pounding commentary, punctuated with the statement, "If the brewery doesn't re-sign Ozzie Smith—they should sell the ballclub!"

It was powerful, and in the era before emails and tweets, I got loads of phone calls from fans who agreed with my passionately-spoken opinion. When I came into work the next day, I was summoned to the office of station boss Allan Cohen.

He said, "I want to talk to you about that commentary."

I was thinking, "Good! It was great!"

Allan didn't think so. He leaned forward from behind his desk. "Do you know how much money Anheuser-Busch *spends in advertising* on this television station?"

I knew ad revenue is important, especially to the boss, and it dawned on me that if Anheuser-Busch pulled its advertising…

I took a deep breath, and looked Allan right in the eye. "I suppose it's probably a *very* large number," I said softly. Then I leaned forward, and in a much more spirited tone, I added, "But if the brewery doesn't re-sign Ozzie Smith, then they SHOULD sell the ballclub!"

They re-signed Ozzie.

HOLDING BACK

While my career was going well, I felt incomplete. Hungering for love and intimacy, I took notice when a new reporter came to work at Channel 4. Judy was from the East Coast—street smart, intelligent, and achingly beautiful. It took me about three months to work up the courage to ask her out. We went to a fine restaurant and everything was going great. Enthralled with the possibility that she could be *the one,* I marched forward.

"Have you ever been married?"

She paused. "Yes. Once. It was horrible."

Not what I was hoping to hear. I rarely dated divorced women. I wanted to find someone for whom marriage would be a new adventure, as it would be for me. I tried to be kind. "If you don't want to tell me about it, that's okay."

She hesitated, but only for a second. "I always figured I would be married forever. But after the wedding I found out he only married me because he wanted to have sex with me."

I gasped. I could not believe that any human being would so *abuse* this beautiful woman solely for his own selfish physical pleasure.

"Did you get an annulment?"

"No, I—uh, no I didn't. The process requires that you almost have to relive what happened and I didn't have the strength to go there." I was sympathetic, but sad at the same time. If Judy got an annulment, I'd certainly be interested in dating her.

At the time, I had a wonderful spiritual director named Father Hilary. He was a manly man. We used to do grueling, four-mile runs on hilly terrain. He was a linebacker in high school, a gifted right-handed pitcher at Notre Dame before an arm injury put an end to his baseball days. I confided in him not only about spiritual matters but about my attempts to find the right woman.

When I told Father Hilary the circumstances with Judy, he opined that she had a likely case for an annulment. I was delighted when he consented to talk to her. Unhappily, she could not bear the agony of documenting what had happened, have the Church contact the jerk who abused her, and whatever else might be a part of the process. She decided not to pursue an annulment.

I was at a crossroads. In principle, this was similar to Saginaw. I could obey God and his Church or I could ignore the Church and pursue Judy. Once again, I chose not to be a hypocrite.

With the end of another potential relationship, I shared with Father Hilary my mantra of "I will become the greatest local sportscaster in America." I even gave him my copy of *Think and Grow Rich.* I was eager to see what he would think of it.

To my surprise and dismay, Father Hilary wasn't very impressed.

"Um, Zip, it's got some nice inspirational stories. There are certainly some good ideas there." Then he looked at me and said, "Regarding your career, if you are not doing it for God, it's a waste."

I thought about Father Hilary's words later, but I was not far enough along on the spiritual path to understand them. My thinking was more along the lines of, *being rich and famous isn't a sin, so why did I have to do it all for God?* I had just given up the most beautiful woman I had ever met to obey Church teachings, but I didn't see a need to bring God into my work life.

HOLDING ON FOR DEAR LIFE

Some really memorable things happened in 1994. O.J. Simpson led America on the longest, slowest police chase in history, *Forrest Gump* dominated the movie scene, and O'Reilly invited me to join the

Men of Adventure. The MOA was a group of guys hand-picked from various periods of Bill's life.

As soon as I accepted, the MOA embarked on a three-day white-water rafting trip on the Rogue River, which runs from the middle of Oregon to the Pacific Ocean. The trip was particularly exciting for me, for two reasons: I had never gone white-water rafting, and I did not know how to swim. Hey, why sweat the small stuff?

There we were, in three rafts, five guys plus a guide in each. Our guide gave me a crash course in rowing and rafting technique, and even more to my liking, he provided us with lifejackets.

For about twenty minutes, I was captivated as we floated along between the hilly, forested river banks, observing elk on land, and osprey flying above it. And then I saw it. A wall of foaming, churning water appeared without warning right in front of us. Suddenly we were fighting for survival—or at least to stay in the raft.

Our craft was thrown into the air but when we hit the waves we managed to stay afloat. The raft that O'Reilly was in, wasn't so fortunate. I turned just in time to see it capsize. We made it through the rapids and landed on a sandbar. O'Reilly's crew survived their unscheduled swim, and somehow made it to the same place. On the shore, O'Reilly and his bearded, mountain man guide colorfully engaged in an exchange about why they all ended up in the drink. Over the next three days, we hit a number of intense rapids, but we never again capsized.

In calm waters, O'Reilly encouraged me to jump into a one-man kayak and paddle alongside the raft. Someone snapped a photo, and a few days later, I showed St. Louis its favorite TV sportscaster looking like one heck of an outdoorsman on the 10pm news.

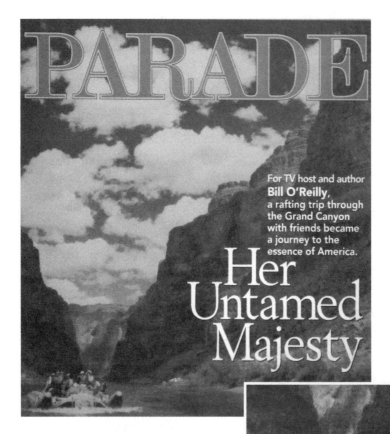

For TV host and author **Bill O'Reilly**, a rafting trip through the Grand Canyon with friends became a journey to the essence of America.

Her Untamed Majesty

The Men of Adventure rafting through the Grand Canyon

Over the next two decades, the Men of Adventure explored some of the most exotic spots in the world. Perhaps the most memorable was invading the Grand Canyon.

The view from the top was awe-inspiring, but we weren't going to just stand there and gawk. We journeyed 9.8 miles down to the Canyon floor, half of us hiking, and half of us on mules. Not wishing to trust *my* life to one of the least intelligent animals on earth, I hiked.

At some points, the descending path was only about six feet wide. One of the MOA had his back pressed against the Canyon wall. He looked ridiculous, but I understood how he felt. There were no guard rails to prevent a multi-thousand foot free fall to death if one ventured over the edge. I decided this would not be a good day for jogging.

The journey took us through the most magnificent natural beauty I have ever seen. The formations and texture and shades of shale and limestone extended as far as the eye could see. It was 55 degrees when we started out. It was 95 degrees when we reached the base of the Canyon four hours later.

After stashing our gear at the Phantom Ranch, we traded stories around the campfire. A couple of young women came over to visit. Recognizing O'Reilly, they went ga-ga for a while. Then things got interesting. The ladies looked at Evan, one of our guys, who was sitting next to Bill. Evan had curly dark hair and a mustache, and the girls thought they recognized him. Well, not exactly *him*.

One of the women said to Evan, "Hey! You're Al Franken!" Franken is the former Saturday Night Live comedian turned U.S. Senator from Minnesota. Franken and O'Reilly can't stand each other. They disagree on everything.

The other woman said, "Yeah, you're Al Franken, but..." Their eyes moved to Bill while her friend finished the sentence.

"...don't you guys *hate* each other?"

Evan was in the mood for fun. "Nah, nah, nah. That's all an act for the cameras. In reality, we're good friends. See, we even vacation together!"

The women's jaws dropped. They thought they had discovered the secret of the century. We tried not to crack up as the women asked for autographs. After a while, one of the ladies' boyfriends showed up, and he wasn't quite sure if Evan was Al. Evan 'fessed up just before we were about to lose it.

For the next three days, we sliced through the Canyon, rafting 165 miles on the Colorado River. We slept tentless on sandbars in our sleeping bags, gazing at the magnificent array of stars while shielding our faces from the blowing sand. Exhilarating.

We capped the Grand adventure with a helicopter ride out of the Canyon.

HANGING ON A LIMB

After leading us on more than twenty years of exciting adventures, O'Reilly has barely tempered the activities. In 2014, the MOA hit the big island of Hawaii, which *sounds* nice and relaxing.

Our 2012 trip was to Iceland, and between the airport and our hotel, Hawaii looked surprisingly similar. The land was covered with dark brown lava spewed forth decades ago from erupting volcanoes. Not a single tree for miles, just acres of lava rocks.

We traveled 25 miles to the Mauna Kea Beach Hotel, a lavish place hewn out of the lava by the Rockefellers back in the 1960s. The promenade featured a world-class fitness center surrounded by high-end shops, restaurants, and an exotic spa. The beach was fabulous, and the ocean water hovered around 70 degrees. Our rooms featured balconies overlooking the ocean and big-screen TVs, but the Men of Adventure weren't going to spend much time inside.

We set out on a new adventure—the sport that bears my name. Zip-lining. *Big-time* zip-lining. The local TV stations were running stories about the zip-lining instructor who had died on the course the day before. But the MOA were undaunted.

We took a 25-minute van ride to a facility where we became "fully equipped." Helmets, harnesses running up through the crotch, heavy gloves so that the tightly-strung steel cables wouldn't rip our hands apart.

We traveled in Swiss army vehicles over terrain so rough we were almost tossed out. Our guides took us onto a platform eight feet off the ground. Hardly scary. But this was just "flight school." We jumped off the platform as gravity propelled us forward, our harnesses clipped onto the cables overhead. We learned to brake with one hand on the cable as we approached the landing station, a small circle of wood built around a large tree trunk.

Naturally, the MOA graduated from school, and that's when the real fun began. We did nine runs, each one higher and higher into, over, and through the heavily-wooded forest. On three occasions, we had to walk on 150-foot swinging rope bridges to get to the next launching pad. It's hard to describe the adrenaline rush of zipping through the air at a speed of 45-miles-an-hour, for about 1100 feet, over lush Hawaiian flowers and streams, and then braking to land, without smacking into a tree. Our adventure concluded with a 30-foot repel to the ground, followed by the Swiss vehicle soiree over the rugged terrain. What a blast!

Part of the joy was doing it with great friends. Friendship is one of the dearest things in life, and I'm forever indebted to O'Reilly for including me in the MOA. What a group. Three guys went to first grade with Bill. A couple of others were his classmates at Marist College. He met Peter Jinman, the British veterinarian/outdoorsman/ pub owner extraordinaire, studying abroad. One guy taught high school with him in a tough section of Miami. TV execs, professionals, a heroic Catholic priest, and various others, Men of Adventure all.

Our friendships *far* exceed connecting on Facebook.

The Men of Adventure relaxing after conquering zip-lining in Hawaii. O'Reilly is in the back row, far left, I'm in the middle of the front row, taking a knee

GRABBING THE MICROPHONE

In the midst of doing hard-hitting commentaries, breaking big stories, researching, writing, producing and performing sportscasts that informed *and* entertained, I created a radio syndication business.

I knew Dick Vitale from my Saginaw days when he was coaching first the University of Detroit, and then the Detroit Pistons, so I gave him a call. By now, he was all the rage on ESPN.

"Hey, Dick, I've got an idea! Why don't you record daily one-minute radio commentaries? You can knock off an entire week of programs in one session! I'll hire some people and we'll syndicate the show all over the country. We'll sell the advertising, and I'll pay *you* a flat fee."

Dicky V liked the idea. For a fee of $80,000.

Suddenly my beautiful home in the St. Louis suburbs turned into the offices of *Radio Personalities Inc.* I hired six bright, young people to come into every available nook and cranny, and call radio stations. We entitled the commentaries, *Dick Vitale, Talkin' Roundball.*

Within weeks, 250 radio stations were carrying the program. Now we needed to sell advertising to cover costs—and Dick's salary—and hopefully make a profit. Unfortunately, the sales people I hired failed to sell. So I decided to take on the challenge.

Some days I would jump on an early morning flight to Chicago, meet with potential sponsors, fly back in the afternoon, and write and perform the 6pm and 10pm sportscasts on Channel 4. Crazy and exhausting? You bet. And the saddest thing was, I failed to sell the advertising.

Undaunted, I sought to expand, rather than contract, *Radio Personalities Inc.* I approached Pro Football Hall of Famer Dan Dierdorf, who lived nearby. Dan was represented by my agent, Art Kaminsky. Art helped Dan land the position of color commentator on ABC's *Monday Night Football.*

"Hey, Dan, Dick Vitale is doing these basketball shows. Why don't you do some football commentaries? You can tape five of them in a session. In fact, you can do them right here in my house. I'll put in a little recording studio."

Well, Dan agreed—for a mere $60,000 a year. He wasn't as demanding as Dick. He told me he'd use the money to put his daughter through college. We labeled the shows, *Offsides with Dan Dierdorf.* As Dan was lighting it up on *Monday Night Football,* the program went over big. More than 400 radio stations picked it up.

Nevertheless, we still had trouble selling the advertising, and I sucked up the losses.

One December night, Vitale thanked me in a unique way for our *Talkin' Roundball* partnership. He was in St. Louis to do the so-called "Battle for the Braggin' Rights" game, the Missouri Tigers vs. the Illinois Fighting Illini. Every year, alumni from the two schools fought for the 20,000 available tickets. A few minutes before game time, while the teams were warming up, the one and only Dicky V put his arm around my shoulder and walked me around the entire periphery of the court, chatting with me as if I was his best friend in the world. To the fans, it made me look like a big-time basketball insider, and a close pal of the most colorful college basketball commentator of all time.

Still, I had problems.

I was making $350,000 a year, but I wasn't saving *anything*. I was paying the fees to Dicky V and Double D, a large chunk was going to taxes, and a smaller chunk to my agent. I had a beautiful home but a large mortgage, and I unwisely chose to drive a luxury car, thinking it might impress wife candidates in the precious few moments I had for dating.

On top of that, I was burned out from working until midnight for 19 years in five cities at six TV stations. I had to plot a way out. Creativity kicked in.

In 1995, I invented *The Great American Sports Trivia Show!*

It was a live, three-hour, Saturday morning radio show where callers from around the USA answered trivia questions. For each correct answer, they got a prize. The first question was always easy, like, "What Major League Baseball team has won the most World Series?" When the caller answered, "The Yankees!" he won an official major league baseball. The second question was tougher, and the prize, bigger. A caller who answered *six* questions correctly, won a *huge* prize, like an all-expenses paid trip to the Super Bowl. To spice it up, we threw in sound effects, music cuts, and fabulous, rare radio sports clips. By the way, this was years before the dawn of *Who Wants to Be a Millionaire.*

I hired my friend, Chuck Neff, a producer of hope-filled, inspirational documentaries, to be our general manager. Chuck brought in Marty Ryan, the former producer of *"The Today Show"* and current producer of *"Fox News Sunday,"* to produce. I was the on-air host.

Radio stations in 57 cities, including New York and Chicago, picked up the show. The only challenge left was to find advertisers. I knew it would help to add a big-name co-host.

GIANT HANDS

I not only came up with a big name, I came up with a big *man.* Kareem Abdul-Jabbar. The NBA's all-time leading scorer, six-time NBA Most Valuable Player, six-time NBA world champion, three-time NCAA champ at UCLA. *Pretty big.*

Kareem had been retired for six years. He had a reputation for being an introvert. He led a private life off the court, and was often described as reticent. For much of his playing career, he had shunned the media. For some reason, I thought I could bring him out of his shell.

I contacted his representatives, and they were excited. I think Kareem was hosting a local jazz radio show, and they viewed a national show as a big step up.

I flew to LA with two of my young techs, Joe and Alan. We found ourselves waiting for Kareem in his living room. Cool. To my young techies, *very* cool. They reacted like schoolgirls when they saw some of the big man's MVP trophies on the mantle. Kareem's reps rolled their eyes.

Somehow, Joe and Alan kept from swooning when Kareem walked in. All 7-foot-2 of him. He was wearing a t-shirt and the longest pair of blue jeans I had ever seen. He was very relaxed as he sat on a couch opposite my chair. His knees were almost at my eye level. I mentioned that we both went to Christian Brothers of Ireland high schools, me at Brother Rice in Detroit, and Kareem at Power Memorial in New York. He nodded. I joked that he no doubt scored a few more points than I did. He barely smiled. I described the concept of the *Great American Sports Trivia Show.*

"Any questions, big guy?"

"Not really."

I had been in broadcasting plenty long enough to know that performers often have different personalities when they are on stage. I was hoping that somehow, someway, Kareem would turn it on when we got into the studio.

Sadly, it didn't happen. As the tape rolled to capture the audition, young Joe went in another studio and impersonated a radio listener calling in to the program. I was my energetic self.

"HI, JOE!!! THANKS FOR CALLING! READY TO WIN SOME PRIZES?"

Joe set the big guy up perfectly. "Yep, sure am. But I'm really just excited to be on the air with Kareem. Kareem, this is a thrill! I was at the game when you won your first NCAA title at UCLA!"

Kareem was silent. I shook my head and motioned for him to

speak into the microphone. He all but whispered, "Nice."

And that's the way the entire audition went. Kareem truly tried, but he was so low-key, that *I* almost fell asleep.

We brought the tape back to St. Louis, but couldn't bear to listen to more than ten minutes of it. It wasn't going to work. I was resigned to host the *The Great American Sports Trivia Show* solo.

The program attracted plenty of listeners each week, and we gave out tremendous prizes—Super Bowl trips, flights and tickets to the All-Star Game, all kinds of stuff. Unfortunately, I was footing the bill, because when the show launched, the Vermont Teddy Bears was our only "major" sponsor.

Each week, I'd travel to the big advertising agencies, but as we fell short of reaching a potential audience of 75% of the country, they gave me the cold shoulder. I wished I would have been walking in with Kareem. Even if he said nothing, we would have had a better chance.

Without sponsorships, the show was doomed. We hung on for nine months, an artistic success, but a *gigantic* financial failure. As the chief investor, I lost all the money that remained from my TV career.

LOSING MY GRIP

Meanwhile, I continued to hunger for love and intimacy.

Friends set me up on dates. One blind date answered her door in a skirt so short, my prevailing thought was, how is she going to sit down? Had this been freshman year in college, I would have been excited. But now I was looking for something more than shapely legs and a pretty face. From a number of bad blind dates, I came to the completely silly conclusion that St. Louis women didn't have enough to offer.

So I headed to Chicago. I spent a couple of vacations living out of a hotel on the Magnificent Mile. Failing to find a love connection jogging along Lake Michigan and pumping iron in the fitness center, I decided to go in a new direction. I'd search for Miss Perfect in Church.

I went to early morning daily Mass at Holy Name Cathedral. Unhappily, most of the Church-goers were businessmen and grey-haired ladies. But one morning Miss Hope appeared. She was kneeling a few rows in front of me on the opposite side of the aisle, dark hair shimmering, stylishly dressed, her face radiant. She received Holy Communion with reverence, so I assumed she was in the good graces of the Church.

As soon as Mass ended, she quickly departed through a side exit. I was sitting closer to the back, so I hurriedly genuflected, pushed open one of the huge main doors, and jogged around the corner. Sadly, my Perfect Woman melted into the busy Chicago streets. Another wife candidate bit the dust.

As soon as I got back to St. Louis, two of my friends *in Chicago* called and told me they had the perfect Chicago woman for me. Wouldn't you know. As it turned out, this woman was not the one, but she introduced me to a friend of hers. I'll call her Sylvia.

Sylvia worked with a cutting-edge health care group. She was a practicing Catholic, and I was attracted to her wit, charm, and intellect. While we didn't see eye to eye on everything, I liked that she could articulate her views with clarity and kindness. I felt like I could talk to her forever. We dated long distance, every other weekend.

Believing that the biggest mistake in life would be marrying the wrong woman, I was always cautious in relationships. Thus, after seeing Sylvia only two weekends a month for five months, I was surprised that I felt *compelled* to propose to her. Strangely, I was completely at peace with the decision. I remember the proposal well.

It was a cold, winter Saturday morning. I took her to the Carmelite monastery in St. Louis, and with majestic snowflakes falling, I walked her through several inches of snow to the statue of Our Lady of Fatima. I reached into my overcoat, and presented her with a red rose. I handed her a card inscribed with a hand-written verse:

> *Roses are red, violets are blue,*
>
> *I love you so much, I want to marry you.*

Okay, so it wasn't T.S. Eliot. She was momentarily confused. She cleared her throat and asked, "What does this mean?" Since she wasn't picking up on it, I asked, "Will you marry me?"

She hesitated for a couple of seconds, which worried me, but then she said, "Yes."

I was on top of the world. We walked back to my car with the snowflakes falling atop her beautiful brown hair, and she looked for all the world like the woman I had always dreamed of. The disappointment of the loss of my radio show, and my money, was off the radar. I was going to get married, start a family, and live a much more sane existence.

Or so I thought.

We signed up for the Catholic Church's mandatory marriage prep program. One of the first components is a written test. I whipped through the questions, no problem, and Sylvia did the same. A week later, the priest who was to marry us called us in and sat us down. He said, "I see a little problem here. Sylvia, on the question that reads, 'Do you trust your fiancé?' you answered, 'No.'" There was an awkward pause in the room. The priest looked at her and said, "I think everybody in St. Louis trusts Zip Rzeppa. What's the problem?" Sylvia answered, "I just have a problem trusting *men*."

The priest recommended psychological testing. We did it in Chicago. The administrator was a highly qualified psychologist in his 18th year on the Archdiocesan marriage tribunal. A week after the test, we reconvened.

To my shock and surprise, the psychologist told us, "I'm going to very strongly recommend that you break off this engagement, and not get married." He said, "Judging by your psychological profiles, I can predict with certainty, that if you do get married, you will be in my office, seeking an annulment, within a short period of time." I was absolutely stunned. I could not believe he could be so certain.

Light was shed when he pulled me aside and said, "Look, I'm doing you a favor here. You scored in the *realm* of psychological normalcy, but your fiancée did not. I'm going to recommend weekly, intense therapy for her, and again, for your own good, I'm telling you, do *not* marry her."

I returned to St. Louis, and after Sylvia and I considered the psychologist's recommendation for some time, we mutually agreed to break off our engagement. I was pleased that she agreed to go into therapy with the psychologist who advised us not to marry.

But you know something? God works in amazing ways. Not only did he bring expert counsel to dear Sylvia, but he also brought together two people in a beautiful, lasting marriage. It just wasn't us.

Let me explain. A week after I proposed to Sylvia, and before we began the marriage prep program, I was hosting my annual, gigantic Super Bowl party. Over the years, the party had grown to about 125 guests, including major St. Louis celebrities, TV personalities, and athletes.

Naturally, I wanted my new fiancée to attend. She was a little intimidated, and I could see her point. She said, "You'll know every single person there, and I will just be 'the fiancée.'"

After thinking for a minute, she came up with an idea. She asked if she could bring a few of her friends to the party. Naturally, I said, "Sure!"

So Sylvia brought in four of her friends from Chicago and another from Kansas City. They were all single women, so I pointed out my eligible guy friends at the party.

I have long forgotten what teams played that day in the Super Bowl, but I will always remember my good friend, Tony Holman, and Sylvia's friend, Teresa, meeting. Tony lived in St. Louis and Teresa lived in Kansas City, but their long distance romance blossomed. Fifteen months after the Super Bowl party, I was honored to attend their wedding, and a little over a year after that, Tony and Teresa founded Covenant Network, which now operates 15 Catholic radio stations and many more translator stations in seven states. Through the years, the programming heard on Covenant Network has touched countless souls, and brought about a well-spring of reversions, conversions, and spiritual renewal.

If Sylvia and I had never gotten engaged, Tony and Teresa, living two hundred miles apart, likely never would have met. God has amazing ways of bringing good out of sorrow. And in retrospect, it's easy for me to believe the psychologist may have been right, and that Sylvia and I may have had great problems, had we married.

Still, the shock and pain of going from planning a wedding to suddenly ending an engagement left me numb. I may not have been clinically depressed, but for a couple of weeks, I barely left the house. I prayed for Sylvia's well-being every day while I experienced the anguish of knowing that I was back to nowhere in my quest to find a bride. I muddled through the painful and ongoing task of informing friends that the engagement was off.

I felt so low. Still numb, I got a call from my mother in Detroit. I'll never forget her words.

GROPING IN THE DARK

"I've got some very bad news for you, Christopher. You know how your dad has been forgetting things? Well, we took him to the doctor, and he gave him these tests, and Dad's been diagnosed with Alzheimer's disease."

I was shocked. I asked, "Mom, are they sure?"

She responded that the tests were definitive and that he'd continue to lose memory and one function after another, until the disease would eventually take his life.

I could barely breathe. One year earlier, at the age of 81, my dad was bowling in a league, and playing 18 holes in the parish golf tournament. Now, the calm, strong force in my corner throughout my entire life was on his way to a long, slow, death.

My life was shrouded in darkness. I thought how much things had changed for me. A year earlier, I had pretty much everything that the world considers important. I was famous and popular, on TV five days a week, making hundreds of thousands of dollars, signing autographs every day. I had a beautiful home in a wealthy suburb. I drove a new luxury car, wore designer clothes, vacationed in Europe.

12 months later, I had given up my TV position, lost my syndicated radio program, lost all the money I had ever earned, lost my fiancée, and now I was going to lose my dad.

God has powerful ways of getting our attention, and at this point, He *certainly* had mine.

HELPING OUT

A SPIRITUAL TOUCH

God needed my attention so He could re-direct my life onto roads *I* never would have taken. The first detour started with a Friday night phone call from a priest whom I did not know. His name was Father Placid Guste, and his words—spoken in an even tone—stuck in my ears.

"Somebody told me you might be interested in helping me do some evangelization in the inner city."

I thought, *this priest has the wrong guy.* I never told *anyone* I was interested in doing evangelization, and if I had, I *sure as heck* wouldn't have suggested that we begin in the inner city.

"Father, what are you talking about?"

After a moment of silence, he said, "Come and see me."

I was confused, but curious. I heard myself reply, "Okay. Tell me where you'd like to meet."

Three days later I was driving in his direction. He wasn't anywhere near the inner city. About 30 miles from the Arch, I turned onto a dirt road at the entrance to Mary the Font Solitude.

I had no pre-conceived notion about where Father lived, but if I had, I never would have envisioned what lay before my eyes. My car kicked up dust in the August heat as I slowly drove past what looked like the Stations of the Cross, nailed onto a row of trees on the left. On the right was a large statue, of whom I was not sure. The grounds were hilly and heavily wooded. I passed strange little huts down off the road in the woods. Each hut was atop cinder blocks. Up ahead stood a modest wood building that appeared to be a chapel. A couple of cars sat about 30 yards from the structure, so I parked alongside.

A priest dressed in a Roman collar and full-length blue cassock appeared, and greeted me with a smile. Somehow I knew I was looking at Father Placid. He welcomed me into his "office," a one room building atop the cinders. I felt like I had entered another world, and spiritually, that was what I was about to do.

Father Placid was the founder of the Society of Our Mother of Peace, and had established a sizeable convent in the Philippines, and a community for men in Nigeria, both of which were steadily producing vocations to the religious life and the priesthood.

He lived at Mary the Font with another priest, five religious brothers, ten nuns, and a smattering of lay people in hermitages. *Hermitages* was what he called the little huts. The community came together to celebrate daily Mass and pray the Liturgy of the Hours. Each member spent an additional *four hours per day* praying in solitude.

I was thinking, *okay, so this is some kind of monastic order.*

Then Father said, "Every afternoon we drive into the inner city," and I gulped, aware that the city was 30 miles away, "and we go into the toughest neighborhoods in the St. Louis archdiocese, and we evangelize."

He looked at me like he was sizing me up. "Would you like to help?"

"Uhhhh, Father," I stammered, "uhhhh, help?"

He said he was looking for lay volunteers to serve in the Society.

"What would that entail, Father?"

There were five aspects. "Spiritual preparation. The first thing is, you must go to Mass every day."

"Every day?"

"Yes. Number two, you must do ten minutes of spiritual reading, every day."

I gave him a nod.

"Three—you must put in thirty minutes of meditative prayer, in silence and solitude, every day." By now, I was grasping this 'every day' thing.

"Four—each Saturday morning, you must come out here for a 90-minute meeting, a kind of group spiritual direction and sharing with other people who are involved, about the progress of the work."

I wasn't sure what 'the work' was, but I wanted to get the total picture. "And, Father, uh—what's number five?"

He barely hesitated, staring me in the eye. "It's the *work*. We send you with a companion into one of the seven poorest parishes in the inner city, and we ask you to get out of your car, walk the streets, knock on doors, cold-call people, and ask them if they'd like to know more about the Catholic Church."

I gulped.

"What do you think?" he asked.

What did I think? My thoughts were all over the place. In an instant, I felt the glow of spending 19 years in TV studios and stadiums and locker rooms, and thought about being a good guy who never missed

Mass on Sunday, and about how so many things had suddenly gone south, and about how no one had ever asked me to do what this unusual priest was sitting here asking me to do.

There was no time to draw up a mental list of pros and cons, to rationally evaluate my aptitude and ability and qualifications, or lack thereof, for doing what he was asking. But in this moment of uncertainty, I really believe the Holy Spirit took over.

I heard myself say, "Sure, Father, I think I'd like to try that."

I exhaled and looked away from Father Placid, bewildered at the words that had just come out of my mouth. But those words were among the most important I ever spoke.

TOUCHED BY A LEPRACHAUN

I began the practices of a lay member of the Society of Our Mother of Peace—daily Mass, daily spiritual reading, 30 minutes of daily meditative prayer. After training for two weeks in the haunting neighborhoods with an experienced door-do-door evangelizer, I was assigned an evangelization partner, a fellow newbie volunteer, a man who was destined to change my life. His name was Declan Duffy.

He openly shared his story. A couple of decades earlier, he and his wife established Dublin's first video store in their native Ireland. Starting out with a handful of movies, they went on to become the Blockbuster of Dublin. Then Declan was stricken with a mysterious illness. He gradually lost the use of his arms and legs and for the next 12 years, he spent life in a wheelchair—when he wasn't in a hospital bed. Doctors tried about 34 different drugs in search of a healing. The eventual diagnosis was multiple sclerosis, for which there is no cure.

Dec became addicted to pain killers as well as alcohol after he and his wife could no longer maintain the video business. He was moved to a hospice for the dying. Pus-filled sores covered his body and he had great pain in swallowing. As a last resort his brother flew him to Lourdes, where, since the appearance of the Blessed Mother to St. Bernadette in 1858, countless cures have taken place. Declan entered the miraculous waters accompanied by a doctor and two nurses, as it was feared he may not survive the cold temperatures.

When they brought him up after immersing him, the sores had miraculously disappeared and he could swallow without pain. He was carried through the streets of Lourdes as people shouted, "A cure! A cure!" But he still could not move his arms and legs. His brother flew him back to Dublin where he was moved from the hospice to a hospital, as there was now hope that he would live.

Six months later, at midnight, a holy man named Andy and a couple of his friends visited. They laid hands on Declan and prayed for a healing from the Holy Spirit. He immediately felt the rush of feeling return to his limbs. The next morning, Dec dumbfounded the doctors by walking for the first time in twelve years. Not long thereafter, he and his wife and their three sons moved to America. In gratitude for his cure, Dec vowed to dedicate the rest of his life to serving those in need.

So here I was—paired up with this holy man to venture into some of the most crime-ridden, drug-infested neighborhoods of St. Louis. We decided it would be a good idea to pray before we hit the streets.

We went to the Chapel of the Holy Spirit Sisters of Adoration, who were better known as the Pink Sisters, because they wore these bright pink habits. They were a cloistered order, but their chapel was open to the public. Two nuns knelt in front of Jesus Christ, disguised as a piece of unleavened bread, resting in a gold monstrance. Declan and I knelt in the back. A security guard, armed with a pistol, sat just outside the entrance.

As we left the chapel, we took comfort in knowing that the Pink Sisters had an armed guard. Declan and I headed out into the streets un-armed, relying on the protection of the Mother of God.

As we went door-to-door, we got all kinds of responses. The neighborhoods were all black, and we were white, and I'm sure some of the residents mistook us for detectives. We'd see the living room blinds open a quarter-inch wide and then quickly shut. Nobody'd come to the door.

Other times, the door would swing open. The homeowner would recognize me from my TV years and shout, "Zip Rzeppa? Wow! Did you come here to put me on *The Zippo Awards?*" He'd look at Declan and say, "Is that your camera man?"

"Uh, not exactly."

We were warmly welcomed into many homes. When you say sincerely that you want to talk about the Lord, there's something innate in people that keeps them from slamming the door in your face. We did have some uncomfortable moments, like when we were sitting on an elderly woman's couch, and she said, "Zip, I wouldn't hang around here, there was a shooting next door just last night."

But we were fearless. Father Placid said that under the protection of Mary, no evangelizer had ever been harmed in the 30 years he and his volunteers had been on the streets.

Actually, the scariest part was the threat posed by dogs. Wild dogs. We soon learned there were no electric fences in the inner city. Declan, the little leprechaun, was about 5-foot-3, and one of the dogs was almost up to his waist. But under our Mother's protection, no canine took a chunk out of our legs.

One day we encountered a bigger threat. We ran into a gang. As we came to the end of a street, six young men came around the corner and stood in front of us. We didn't notice any crosses or crucifixes, just a full exhibition of tattoos under red clothing. The look in these young toughs' eyes seem to say, "Who the hell are these guys?" They seemed baffled that two middle-aged white dudes would be wandering their streets. So there we were, pint-sized Declan, and me at 5-foot-9, outnumbered three-to-one. Any physical confrontation was not going to end well.

Dec immediately engaged the gang members in friendly conversation, chatting with them in his strong Irish brogue. If his stumpy little appearance hadn't surprised them, his accent certainly took them aback. I quickly tried to conjure up a fake Irish brogue in my head, but Dec didn't need my help. He popped questions about God at our brothers, and to my amazement, the gang members responded with thoughtful replies.

Now, the replies ranged from "Why you wanna talk about God?" to "I never think about God," to "My momma used to talk to Him all the time," but almost instantly, we found ourselves engaged in a discussion about the Lord and Satan, life and death, Heaven and hell, that lasted probably a full ten minutes before the gang decided to move on down the street. Physically, we were no match for a gang, but spiritually, the little leprechaun, filled with the Holy Spirit, had taken control.

Now, I wouldn't bet that those gang members rushed to the Baptismal font in the next few days, but I know it's possible our little chat *may* have led them to think about the Almighty sometime. We had planted the seeds.

REAPING THE HARVEST

I vividly remember seeds planted by another coming to fruition. We were invited into the home of a 73-year-old woman named Jesse, who was, for the most part, bed-ridden. She told us, with great fondness, how this priest, Father Bob, had been so wonderful to everyone in the neighborhood, riding his bike up and down the street, bringing good cheer to the neighbors. When her husband died, Father Bob hosted the post-funeral reception at his parish center, even though neither Jesse nor her deceased husband was Catholic.

We asked her, "How long ago was that?"

"Ohhh, about six years ago."

The Spirit led Declan to ask, "Jesse, have you ever thought about becoming Catholic?"

Jesse replied, "Well, yes I have, and I think this might be a good time."

We tried to keep our jaws from dropping. A conversion in the making!

Since Jesse was unable to go to RCIA (the Rite of Christian Initiation for Adults) because of her health, one of the nuns from the Society of Our Mother of Peace came to Jesse's home a number of times, and using words, books, and videos, prepared her to be received into the Catholic Church.

That spring, at the Easter Vigil, Declan and I became the Godparents of 73-year-old Jesse, and her 15-year-old grandson, and her 5-year-old granddaughter. The grandson became an usher at their parish, and the granddaughter sang in the children's choir. We simply reaped the fruits of the seeds planted by the bicycle-riding priest, Father Bob Gettinger, who has toiled for souls for years in serving the poor.

We went door-to-door, one day per week, *every* week, two hours at a time, in murderous heat, extreme cold, sunny days, rainy days, all kinds of weather, for the next year until health and family issues forced Declan to stop. I continued to evangelize for another three years with different door-to-door partners. It was the work of the Lord.

THE HANDS OF INNOCENCE

Early in our evangelization days, Dec asked if I had a job. He had lived the first 40 years of his life in Ireland, and had missed all 8,000 of my TV sportscasts. Humbling. I filled him in on what I *used* to do. Dec listened, smiled and said, "Want to see where I work?"

He drove me to this 100-year-old, seven-story, red brick building in the city. It was the home of the Metropolitan Employment and Rehabilitation Service agency, better known as MERS. I was amazed at what I saw inside its ancient walls. The mission of MERS was to help people with mental and/or physical disabilities and challenges to find employment. The building was teeming with people in need.

We took the elevator to the top floor, which housed women coming out of prison, women looking to transition back into the work world with a felony record and no recent job experience. One floor below, professionals instructed the blind and the deaf, the vision-impaired and the hearing-impaired. On another floor, counselors assisted victims of head trauma accidents. On another level, about 40 people, primarily men, worked toward HVAC accreditation, so that they could land jobs in the heating and cooling industry.

The second floor was a sheltered workshop for those whose disabilities were so severe that they were not candidates for the outside work world. But they were *working*, performing simple, repetitive tasks such as packing boxes and sealing and stamping envelopes. We concluded the tour in the cafeteria which doubled as a training ground for a dozen people who wanted to work in the restaurant industry.

After the eye-opening grand tour, Declan said, "So what do you think? Would you like to work here?"

I was taken aback. Still numb from the collapse of my national radio show, I wasn't really looking for a job. And if I had been, it wouldn't have been here. I shook my head. "This place is incredible, Dec, but it's, uh—social work. My training is in journalism. I'm a broadcaster."

Dec replied, "Yes! Which means you could help our people—get jobs! Employers would listen to a pitch from you."

I rolled my eyes, but Dec gently pushed forward. "Listen, when I go into a company, I beg them to give our disabled clients a chance. I plead with them to just give our people a *try-out*. And oftentimes what I get in response is, 'Well, we'll think about it. We've got your card, *Del-can*. We'll call you.' And most of them never do." And then Dec got an Irish twinkle in his eye. "But if they've seen you on *television*"—he said 'television' as if it was the moon, or something—"well, I bet you'd get a much different response."

I couldn't deny the possibility. I knew some people might even ask for autographs.

The following week, I accepted a full-time position at MERS as a job developer, assigned to assist those with disabilities to find employment. My starting salary was $22,500, a slight dip from the $350,000 I made in TV land.

As I threw myself into learning a new field, the sports media writer for the St. Louis Post-Dispatch got wind of my career switch, and came to MERS to do a story. He wrote that I had gone from working in the state-of-the-art, downtown studios of Channel 4 in the shadow of the Arch, to a building that didn't even have mirrors in the men's room. Well, in truth, we *did* have mirrors, but not a whole lot more.

But I wasn't there looking for ambience. The Lord, through Declan and a host of dedicated, underpaid counselors, trainers, and professionals, was about to teach me to serve. More completely, He was about to break my heart of stone, and give me a heart for the poor.

I did not think of myself as a bad guy; I just spent a lot of time doing things to please myself. At MERS, the Lord showed me a much different way to live. He blessed me with a job where those I served walked slower, talked slower, or thought slower. The Lord had to *slow everything down for me,* so I could begin to see Him in others.

As my eyes were opened to see the presence of the Lord in all these beautiful people with disabilities, I soon began to see Him in all people. Truly, deeply life-changing.

TOUCHING OTHERS

I cannot adequately express how deeply I came to love those I served, but I can share a couple of their stories. One night, Declan and his wife were in the checkout line at Walmart, and in front of them was a woman in a wheelchair who had multiple disabilities. She had multiple sclerosis, which limited the use of her arms and legs; she was legally blind; she could not speak intelligibly; and she was incontinent. She was assisted by a staff member from her group home.

Declan said to his wife, "You know, I'd like to work with somebody like that someday." Well, the woman in the wheelchair checked out and so did Dec and his wife, and he didn't think anything further about it.

But God works in strange and marvelous ways. The next morning when Declan came into MERS, he found the woman in the wheelchair, sitting in his office. She said, "I heard you help people get jobs, could you help me?"

Dec smiled and said, "Sure."

He called me in, as we often worked as a team. The woman's name was Kim. She was represented by Rehabilitation Services for the Blind. So we called that agency to ask for a referral for job development. We were surprised when the Rehab person said, "We're not going to give you a referral. Kim is 40 years old, she's got multiple disabilities, she's never had a job in her life, and we don't think she can do it."

Declan immediately challenged that opinion. "Look, it's nine o'clock in the morning. She got up to the third floor of this old building, she got to my office, and she's brimming with a can-do attitude. We'd like to give it a shot."

Reluctantly, Rehabilitation Services for the Blind gave us a 30-day contract to work with Kim. Dec and I looked at each other, and began to brainstorm areas where Kim might be able to work—*and* succeed. We knew that she could get to Walmart because she was there the night before. Walmart had a greeter's position open.

We took Kim over in Dec's van, and guided her through the mandatory interview process. We saw that some adjustments would have to be made. Walmart was less concerned about Kim's wheelchair than her incontinence.

So as we often did for our clients with disabilities, we carved the job description to fit the client. The position was four hours per day, so we got Walmart to reduce it to two hours, so they wouldn't have to worry about bathroom issues. And glory be to God, after some enthusiastic pushing from Dec and I, Walmart agreed to hire Kim. Grace was flowing.

Kim's start date was set for the following Tuesday. But the day before, we got a call from her home. The group home manager asked us to tell Walmart that Kim was *not* going to show up. Naturally, we asked why. The manager replied "Well, we've been thinking—if Kim takes this job, we'll have to get her and her wheelchair into the van, drive her to Walmart, get her and the chair out of the van and into the store, and then we'll have to go back and pick her up, and get her home, and we just think it's too much."

For a moment, Declan and I were speechless. But only for a moment. We were on a speaker phone, as was the group home, and Kim was present. So I said, "Kim, what do *you* think?"

I will never forget her reply as long as I live. In her slow, halting, garbled voice, Kim said, "Zip, we're…going…to…do……..whatever…it…takes."

So I said to the group home manager, "Hey, you're *paid* to serve Kim! You get her in that van, and we'll see you over at Walmart tomorrow morning at 10 o'clock." So they got her in the van and got her in the door at Walmart. We had our very best job coach waiting to assist her, to orient her, to instruct her, to help her for the first few days on the job. And using the only perceivable talents that she had—her smile, her spirit, and a not-to-be-denied, can-do attitude—Kim began greeting the customers coming through the doors of Walmart.

And she flourished.

Some customers may have had trouble discerning her words, but they couldn't miss the smile on her face and the joy in her presence.

After 30 days, Rehabilitation Services for the Blind sent reps to check things out. They were amazed to see Kim smiling and greeting the customers. Suddenly, they reversed field and began throwing money at the case. They bought Kim a ChatBox to attach to her wheelchair so that, with the one good finger on her one functioning hand, Kim could hit a key that would prompt an electronic voice to say, "Hello, welcome to Walmart!" Another key prompted, "Is that an exchange?" And another, "The restrooms are to the left." In all, 16 keys were programmed to say anything Kim needed to serve the customers.

Kim kept the job for a glorious three-and-a-half years. Then she contracted a kidney disease. Her dear little body couldn't fight it off, and she passed away.

Sometimes when I'm feeling down, I think of Kim and her sweet smile, and how in those three-and-a-half years, this woman whom people did not think could work, had touched the lives of not hundreds, but *thousands* of people who came through the doors of Walmart.

Kim proved that what the world considers disabilities are really spiritual gifts. God speaks *very slowly* through these people's lives about the value of joy and simplicity. I began to see that my fast operating brain was filled with too much static to understand and appreciate what is truly essential in life.

CARRYING A TUNE

I was privileged to assist a man named Jim. Jim was huge, about 6-foot-4, and he weighed well in excess of 300 pounds. We helped him get a job as a part-time security guard, and in his uniform, he certainly looked the part. Since his thinking process wasn't always *crystal clear,* we strongly advised the security company to limit Jim to *un-armed* assignments.

Jim liked being a security guard, but he had a bigger dream. He wanted to be a singer. Well, at MERS, we always tried to make dreams come true! I invited Jim to my office.

I asked Jim about his dream. He said, "I want to sing on *The Merv Griffin Show.*"

I stifled a chuckle. "Jim, Merv's been off the air for quite a few years."

He pondered that for a moment. "Well—then I want to sing on *The Tonight Show with Jay Leno.*"

"Do you have any CDs out?"

"No."

"Then, Jim, that's not going to happen."

I watched as my words seemed to crush him. "Jim, Jim, Jim, uh—do you have a tape of yourself singing?"

"Sure." He pulled a cassette out of his pocket. I popped it into a player. It was Jim, singing the Star Spangled Banner, *a capella.* He sounded pretty darn good. Not quite Susan Boyle, but his big, deep, booming voice was impressive.

I harkened back to my earlier career. I called the communications director of the St. Louis Cardinals. "Hey, I've got an anthem singer for you."

Anthem singers were booked for the remainder of the season.

Undaunted, I called the NHL's St. Louis Blues. "Hey, I've got an anthem singer for you."

The Blues said, "Zip, thanks—but no thanks."

Dropping down in scale, I called St. Louis' indoor soccer team, the

Ambush. Same pitch.

The Ambush PR guy replied, "Zip, here's our philosophy on the anthem: we have somebody different sing it before every game, and if they sing great, great! And if they don't—well, okay! Let's play soccer."

I almost dropped the phone. "Jim and I are on our way over to see you!"

We went in and played Jim's tape, and the PR guy said, "Wow! Okay Jim, you can sing the national anthem before our game on Sunday night, November 4th."

As we drove back to MERS, Jim was higher than a kite. We went into my office, and I dug out the Ambush schedule. I looked at the date, and almost fainted.

"Ohhhh, no. Uh, Jim?"

"What's the matter?"

"Uh, on November 4th, St. Louis is playing *Montreal*." I looked Jim in the eye and asked, "My friend, have you ever sung the *Canadian* national anthem?"

"No. Why?"

I wondered how this could possibly work. The Montreal game was two weeks away. In the age before the Internet, I sent Jim to the library to find the words to the Canadian national anthem.

He went home and practiced and practiced and practiced.

On the night of the game, Jim walked out to the microphone at the center of the playing surface. As the crowd stood up, they turned out all the lights in the arena and put a spotlight on Jim.

I took a deep breath and whispered a prayer for our client.

Jim sang the Canadian national anthem *flawlessly*. And then, as if on cue, he turned his massive physique to the American flag, and with all his heart and soul, he *belted out* the Star Spangled Banner. The lights came up, the crowd cheered, and I looked into the stands. My eyes found Jim's mother and his older brother. They were crying. I was fighting to hold back *my* tears. And that night, Big Jim walked off that field with more confidence in his step than I had ever seen. A great moment!

But the story of Jim doesn't end there. A couple of months later, he called and said, "You know, singing at that soccer game was great, but I really would like to sing before a Cardinals game at Busch Stadium."

Oh, boy. Here we go again. Another opportunity to make Jim's dream come true! I called the Cardinals, and they told me that their sales department was now handling the anthem. Well, I pitched the idea to sales person Julie Mitchell, and she said, "Zip, here's the deal. If your group can sell 500 tickets to a mid-week game in August against San Diego, your client can sing the national anthem on the field before the game."

I could hardly believe my ears. I paused for effect, gazed into Julie's eyes, and said, "You get me those tickets."

I whipped together a meeting of our big-hearted, hopelessly underpaid professionals who were so dedicated to help the challenged. I laid out the story. "Come on, guys! We can sell 500 tickets! And then Big Jim gets to sing at Busch Stadium!"

They were all in. We divided up the tickets and for the next two months, we tried to sell them to our neighbors, our mothers, our brothers, people on the street, anybody. Two days before the game, we sold the last of the 500 tickets. I pounded out the Cardinals' phone number, got Julie Mitchell, and said, "We did it! All the tickets are sold! Our guy, Jim, gets to sing, right?"

It was music to my ears when I heard her say, "Right!"

You think God doesn't work in strange and marvelous ways? The night before the game, The Cardinals' Mark McGwire hit his 499th career home run. We know now that quite a few of those dingers were aided by performance-enhancing substances, but at the time, not many had any idea. So it was a big deal that the game at which Jim was to sing turned out to be the first game in which McGwire would have a chance to hit his 500th home run. All of St. Louis wanted to witness it.

When I arrived at MERS the morning of the game, I had thirty messages waiting for me. They all said pretty much the same thing: "Hey, you got any more of those tickets?"

I drove Jim to the ballpark. He'd be singing the national anthem in front of a capacity crowd of 47,000 people. As always, Jim wanted to sing *a cappella*—no organ, no music track, no nothing—just Jim.

To support the big guy, they let me stand on the field. A Cardinals employee carried out a microphone stand and placed it at home plate. Just like at the soccer game, I was praying for our client.

The public address announcer asked the 47,000 fans to stand and remove their hats, and then he introduced Jim. The crowd hushed, and Jim began to sing. I was so proud of him. His big, strong voice boomed out over the Busch Stadium loudspeakers which resounded with his rendition of The Star Spangled Banner.

But about halfway through the anthem, Jim suddenly forgot the lyrics. He stopped singing, and started to mumble under his breath. I gulped. I was petrified. Someone was going to have to finish the anthem, and I can't sing. Well, after a couple of seconds, something clicked in Jim's brain. He nodded his head, and somehow picked it up right where he left off. He finished the anthem with gusto.

The crowd knew Jim was a client of MERS, and they gave him a big hand. They didn't care that he had messed up. They were waiting to see Mark McGwire. But I'm fretting about our client. Here it was, the biggest moment of his life, and he goofed it up. I'm wondering how it was going to affect him, not just this night, but for the next week—and for the rest of his life.

I was standing by the screen. Jim left the microphone and walked his 300-plus pounds right up to me. He looked me in the eye and said, "Oooops—oops, oops, oops."

I have no idea how I kept from cracking up.

Julie Mitchell came rushing over, and said, "Jim! That was a great recovery!"

I chimed in, "Yeah, and your voice sounded great over the loud-speakers!"

Big Jim looked at Julie, then he looked at me, and said, "I only have one question." We waited as he paused. "Does this blow any chance I have of singing the anthem at a Cardinals game next year?"

We did all we could to keep from laughing. Julie kindly told Jim the Cardinals would consider bringing him back. I walked with Jim up to the section where our 500 ticket buyers had their eyes on Jim. In his booming voice, he said, "Well, I blew it." After a pause, he added, "But it's a great night for baseball! I think McGwire's gonna do it tonight. Let's have a good time!"

I was in awe of his humility and spirit. If *I* had forgotten the words in front of 47,000 people, I would have hid in a men's room stall for the rest of the night. But there was Jim, encouraging all of us to have fun. Beautiful!

By the way, McGwire hit his 500th home run that night, and his 501st, as well, so we all had a good time. And the next season, the Cardinals invited Jim back to sing—and he sang the anthem perfectly.

CASH IN HAND

Tom Schuchardt was the head of our department at MERS. He was a big man who walked with a noticeable limp, but his mind was sharp and his heart was huge. He'd been serving others for years. On my one-year anniversary, he called me into his office.

"Zip, we're going to give you a raise."

"Wow. Great!"

"You're making $22,500."

"Yes."

"We're very happy with your work. We're giving you a raise to $23,100."

I swallowed, and somehow managed to say, "Thank you." Tom wasn't being stingy. That's all his budget would allow for a second-year job developer.

I left his office, recalling some of the huge raises I had received in TV. But I wouldn't trade those raises for what I was doing now. I knew I was called to serve at MERS.

Ironically, I got a very large raise a few months later without asking for it.

The MERS president, Dr. Lew Chartock, a brilliant, clever, native New Yorker, had found an opportunity to start a halfway house for men. The catch was, 75% of the businesses within a three-block radius had to sign an agreement that they were okay with MERS bringing a halfway house into the neighborhood.

Dr. Lew knew there was little chance the businesses would agree, but he challenged his director of operations, Dave Kutchback, to find a way. Dave was a wonderful man. He and his wife, Mary, were pillars of their parish. They had eight kids, and fostered three more. Dave exuded kindness and wisdom, and had the respect of the entire staff.

He came into my office and told me of the challenge. I gulped.

"So, Dave, let me see if I've got this right. You and I are going to walk into the surrounding businesses and say, 'Hi, we work at MERS. You wouldn't mind if we start a program to bring in 50 convicted felons to live in the neighborhood, would you?'"

Dave chuckled. "That's pretty much it, but we wouldn't frame it that way. We just need to get them to sign off on it."

"Oh, sure. So we say, 'Mr. Businessman, just sign on the dotted line, and we'll start moving the felons in.'"

"Zip, we'll present it a little *differently*. Lew is insisting that I find a way to get this done."

I nodded, thinking, *there's no way* we're going to get this done.

We walked into the nearest area business, flashing pleasant smiles. Dave opened.

"Hi, I'm Dave Kutchback, the director of operations at MERS. You know, we're right around the corner. And this is Zip Rzeppa..."

The business owner's jaw dropped. He reached out and started pumping my hand. "I watched your sportscasts for years! You were my all-time favorite! My kids used to beg me to let them stay up and watch *The Zippo Awards* on Friday nights. I can't believe I'm meeting you. What can I do for you, Zip?"

He waved his associates into his office to meet me as Dave smoothly stated that we ran all these wonderful programs to help people with disabilities to find employment, including a halfway house for women that had been trouble-free since its inception, and now we just wanted to start a program to help men who would work hard in rehab to earn their way back into the work-force.

I think the guy may have only been half-listening, but he looked at Dave, beamed a smile at me, and said, "That sounds great." He signed the agreement, then asked for my autograph. It went pretty much the same with the other neighboring businesses. We came back with 100% of the signatures.

Dr. Lew was pleased yet curious to know how we did it. Dave gave me the credit. As Lew was from out-of-town, he had never seen me on TV. But a few days later, he promoted me to MERS vice-president and put me in the office right next to his.

In my new position, I made speeches on behalf of those with disabilities, and assisted Lew on various projects. His favorite thing was using me to quash the occasional evil intentions of other not-for-profits.

If another agency was unfairly or unethically competing for a grant, Lew would call me into his office and get the head of that agency on the phone. I didn't have to say a word.

"You know, pal, I've got *Zip Rzeppa* sitting right across from me. He's got a lot of close friends in TV. You wouldn't want *every investigative reporter in St. Louis* looking into what you're trying to do, would you?" They always backed down.

Lew orchestrated the MERS merger with Goodwill Industries, and grew the Goodwill Stores from 12 locations to more than 40. Revenue to serve those in need increased ten-fold. I learned *a lot* about the not-for-profit world from Lew.

A FEEL FOR THE SPIRITUAL

While I served those in need, my enlightenment was spurred by spiritual reading.

Father Placid insisted that I read Thomas Merton's 1948 autobiography, *"The Seven Storey Mountain."* I don't like reading long books, and this one was about 460 pages, but I read it with great interest. It's been called a 20th century version of St. Augustine's *"The Confessions,"* the story of a brilliant, worldly man who evolved into a contemplative and spent the last years of his life as a Trappist monk, influencing the world through his writing before his sudden death at age 48.

Next, I read Merton's *"No Man Is An Island"* and *"The Seeds of Contemplation."*

My mother loved books, and she sent me *"Heliotropium."* Written in Germany by a Jesuit priest, Father Jeremias Drexelius, in the year 1627, I was impressed it was still in print.

One of its salient points is that nothing happens outside of God's Will. You better believe that gave me something to think about! Good ol' Father Drexelius wrote that God always Wills what is best for us, but because we often live our lives contrary to what God would like to see us choose, he often allows evil, calamity, disaster, hardship, heartbreak, unemployment—you name it—to come into our lives as a way to get our attention, so He can draw us back to Him.

This fascinated me. For my entire life, I had thought I was in control. I was a living, breathing human being, I could choose to do what I wanted, and nobody could stop me in the attempt. God's Will? I hardly thought about it.

I was on the verge of a surge in spiritual growth.

A sentence in a book by the late controversial Jesuit priest, Father Anthony DeMello, affected me to no end. He wrote, "If you look at a tree, and see a tree, you haven't seen the tree. If you look at a tree and see a miracle, *then*, you've seen the tree."

I remember sitting in silence, meditating about this, and then I all but ran out to see if I could "see" the tree at the end of my driveway.

It was a huge oak, I'm guessing about 150 years old. I sought to "see" the tree. I looked at the bottom of the trunk. I knew that a tree has roots and, as I gazed at the ground, I could only imagine how far into the earth this giant oak's roots ran. Now, I am not a botanist or an arborist, and I never did very well in science, but I figured that the rain must come down into the earth, and somehow get soaked up by the roots, which I figured must shoot life and nourishment up the trunk of the tree, all the way into the limbs. I have no idea if that's scientifically correct, but that's was I was surmising.

As my eyes moved upward, I noticed the thick bark, and I marveled how this bark had protected the tree from all the extreme heat, frigid cold, thunderstorms and tornados that had occurred on this spot over the last century-and-a-half. My eyes moved to the tree limbs. Many were pointing in an upward direction, and I could not help but think of the Creator above.

The leaves on the tree were green, as it was springtime. A leaf had fallen to the ground. I picked it up, and marveled at the texture of the leaf, and at the veins running through it. I took in its deep green color, and its fresh smell. I turned it over to discover a different shade of green, a new texture, and the same pattern of veins mirrored from the other side. I stared at the complexity and beauty of this one leaf. Looking up, I tried to guess how many leaves, each of them unique, hung on this tree. It was futile. Hundreds? No, certainly thousands, but how many? I was powerless to know.

I knew people could create fake trees that are on display in homes and offices all over the place, but in an instant I was acutely aware that no high-falutin manufacturing company could create a single tree as big and magnificent as this oak. And that while fake tree manufacturers create beautiful green leaves, they cannot make those leaves change color, drop off, and be replaced by new leaves the following season.

As a gentle breeze began to blow, the countless leaves on this giant oak began to dance. I took a deep breath. I understood that I wasn't looking at a tree. I was looking at a *miracle*.

A TOUCH OF TENDERNESS

In 1998, Declan and I formed a Prayer Group that met the first Monday of each month in my living room. It began with six people, among them, Dec's brother, Ray, a super-successful executive with an international paper company, and Bonnie Coury, the wife of St. Louis Rams wide receivers coach, Dick Coury. I met Dick and Bonnie in my Boston days when Dick was coaching there. He and Bonnie are the sweetest people.

Declan, a fabulous guitar player with an enchanting, raspy Irish voice, would lead us in song. My favorite tune was a short prayer we would sing three times, very slowly. The lyrics were simple, yet profound.

> *Come, Holy Spirit, we need You,*
> *Come, Holy Spirit, we pray.*
> *Come with Your strength and Your Power, Lord,*
> *Come in Your own special way.*

As Dec put away his guitar, we'd break out our Rosary beads, and I'd lead us in Mary's great meditative prayer about her life and that of her Son. We'd reflect on the readings for the upcoming Sunday Mass, and share about issues in the community and in our own lives.

The Prayer Group doubled in size, and then tripled, and by the fourth year 30 to 35 people were coming. One attendee was Colleen Carroll Campbell, who became a brilliant presidential speech writer, author, columnist, and TV host. A youthful businessman attended for a couple of years, quit his profession, entered the seminary, and became a diocesan priest. But the most memorable attendees were a middle-aged woman transported in her wheelchair by a daily Communicant, and the woman's 86-year-old grandmother.

We listened in stunned silence as these women shared their story. Many years ago, the woman in the wheelchair, Sue, was a beautiful teenager, riding home from her high school prom in the back seat with her date, when her date tried to rape her. Sue's friend in the front seat tried to jump into the back to save Sue. But the friend inadvertently bumped the driver, who had been drinking, and the car catapulted off the road, into a tree. Three of those in the car suffered minor injuries, but Sue was severely injured.

At the hospital, days of tests were conducted as Sue remained in a coma. Her grandmother, Betty, was in Sue's room when the doctor delivered the diagnosis.

"I'm very sorry. She's going to be a vegetable."

Betty recoiled, and shouted at the doctor. "A vegetable? A *vegetable?* A vegetable is a potato—corn is a vegetable!" She pointed toward Sue and screamed at the doctor, "*That's* not a vegetable. That's a human being! That's my granddaughter!"

Weeks later, Sue opened her eyes, but weeks of procedures produced very little progress in mental or physical functioning. The recommendation was to put her in a full-care facility, without rehabilitation, as her case was deemed hopeless.

But it wasn't hopeless to Betty. She defied the medical staff and transported her granddaughter to her farm. This widow who had no medical or therapy training created her own methods of rehab. The first components were love and faith. She poured them in, constantly whispering into Sue's ear that she was going to get well. Betty followed up with a massive dose of determination. She placed Sue on the floor, and then slowly but firmly, she stretched out one leg, and then the other. She did the same with Sue's arms. With her caring hands, Betty deeply massaged Sue's entire body, not once, not twice, but three times each day. For weeks. And months. And years.

Ten years after the accident, Betty, filled with love in her heart and fire in her soul, took Sue back to see the doctor who had diagnosed her. Sue was able to wheel herself into the doctor's building. She had regained her bodily functions, and had complete use of her arms and upper body. Her eyes were clear, and her face was radiant. Her speech was a tick slow, but strong and understandable. Showing up without an appointment, Betty demanded to see the doctor. Sue wheeled herself into his office as Betty glared at the man. She pointed to her granddaughter and said, "There's your vegetable!"

The doctor had no idea what Betty was talking about. So Betty recounted the story and reminded him of his words from ten years ago.

"There's your vegetable, Doctor!"

The doctor refused to believe that the pretty woman in the wheelchair was the person he had diagnosed. "That's not possible. This is not the same woman."

Strangely, this was not the first time that Betty had rescued Sue when another could not see the value of her life.

The day after Sue was born, Betty got a call from her daughter, Janice. Janice was a young, frightened, unmarried teen who felt she could not take care of the newborn. In an act of desperation, she placed Sue out in the garage to die.

Betty raced over to her daughter's house. Her daughter was not home. Betty found baby Sue in a pail on the garage floor. She picked her up, wrapped her in a blanket, and drove her to her farm. That day Betty became the de facto mother of Sue, and lived with her the rest of her life.

In a way, Betty was paying forward the kindness of others. Betty herself had been orphaned as an infant in Independence, Missouri. The nuns in a nearby monastery took her in and provided her with food, shelter, nourishment—and love—for the first six years of Betty's life.

IN THE HANDS OF OUR MOTHER

Growing in spiritual fervor, I decided to consecrate myself to Jesus through Mary. The method of Total Consecration taught since the early 1700s has been called a *prayer marathon.*

I decided to go the distance.

Having put myself through extreme physical training to become a college basketball player, I threw myself into intense spiritual training.

My coach was the 18th century priest, St. Louis de Montfort, and my training manual was his *True Devotion to Mary.*

According to de Montfort, St. Augustine taught that the world was unworthy to receive the Son of God directly from the Father's hands, so God gave Jesus to Mary in order that the world would receive the Savior through her.

De Montfort teaches that in return, we should go to the Lord *through* His Mother.

The training consisted of 33 days of preparation. The exercises of the first 12 days were to free me from the spirit of the world—a spiritual detox diet to enable me to shed the fat of my ambition and selfish passions.

The next seven days were about gaining knowledge of myself. Just as I assessed my strengths and weaknesses on the basketball court, I looked with honesty at my virtues and flaws. I felt the burn of humility as God stretched me beyond my pride.

The following week I learned about the sublime virtues of the Blessed Mother, and how she could mold and sculpt the muscles of my interior life.

The final seven days of training brought it all together. The source of my strength is Jesus, and my Mother Mary lifted me like a little child into His loving arms.

At the end of the 33 days, I prayed the prayer of Total Consecration. I continue to renew my Consecration with the words, "I am all Thine and all that I have belongs to Thee, O my sweet Jesus, through Mary, Thy holy Mother."

FINGER ON THE TRIGGER

My search for a wife continued.

I was excited when I found a woman runner to date. Caitlin was one of the fastest female runners in the area. I took her to dinner at a nice restaurant. It was a lovely summer night, so we decided to stroll through Forest Park, which, by the way, is bigger than New York's Central Park. We were out on the grass getting to know each other, exchanging information about our respective lives, nothing touchy-feely, but just nice. All of a sudden, we heard a voice in the darkness.

"Okay, you two lovers. I've heard enough. Zip, is that you?" I was stunned because the voice sure as hell wasn't one that I recognized. The man's next words riveted us to attention.

"Seen you on TV, Zip. I'm over here. Can you see the gun?"

I could barely see a figure lying on the ground in the shadows. I could *not* see a gun. My body tensed up as my mind raced.

He spoke again, with more intensity. "I said, can you see the gun?"

I feared that if I said, "No," he might shoot one or both of us just to let us know he had one. So I said, "Yeah, I see it," even though I didn't.

He said, "Okay, Zip. You're gonna help me out. Let's have your wallet, Zip. Throw it over here." So I threw him the wallet.

"What else you got, Zip?"

I said, "I got nothin', man."

"What about that watch?"

I said, "Listen, pal, my dad gave me this watch."

He said, "That's alright, Zip. Throw it over here." He said, "Now, I don't want any funny business, Zip."

I said, "If you shoot me, do you know how big the manhunt is gonna be for you, pal?"

He said, "Zip, they'll never get me, because they don't know who I am."

The only thing I wanted to do was get out of the park with Caitlin, alive. So I threw him my watch, and said, "Look, you've got all I've got. We're taking off."

He said, "Okay, Zip, start walking. Don't run, walk." And so we did, to the lighted edge of the park, aware that it was possible that at any second, he could shoot one or both of us. Fortunately, no shots were fired. We got to the lighted sidewalk, hurried to my car and drove a few miles away to get a drink. Not exactly the kind of first date I had in mind.

Somehow, Caitlin agreed to go out with me again. Sadly, we didn't have too much in common outside of running—well, that and almost getting shot in Forest Park—and my dream of marrying a fellow runner came to an end.

TOUCHED BY DOCTORS

My mother, knowing that I was attracted to intelligent women, set me up on a date with an oncologist. My mom had sold her a house. I appreciated that the doc was working to find a cure for cancer, but I didn't feel any passion.

A marriage broker matched me up with a thoracic surgeon in Detroit. We dated long distance for two or three weekends, and then she told me she thought we should get married. I was taken aback. I told her I'd like to spend a little more time dating so we could get to know each other better, and to my surprise, she said, "Look, I'm not getting any younger here. If you don't think you're ready to marry me, then I'm moving on."

I let her go.

Later I had a serious relationship with a doctor in St. Louis. She was a brilliant, cardiothoracic surgeon. Her specialty was lungs. When a lung donor passed away within a thousand miles, she'd race to the airport and fly on a specially-equipped jet to the body of the deceased. Time was of the essence. She'd remove the lungs, fly them back to St. Louis, and assist in a lung transplant. Wild and wonderful stuff.

We had quite a number of terrific dates. We got along great. But the big thing that we disagreed on was pretty important. *She did not believe in God.* When she first told me she was an atheist, it was hard for me to believe. Here was a woman who knew more about the miracle of human life and the human body than anyone I could imagine. A woman who dealt *intimately* with the living, the dying, and the dead. A woman who literally saved lives. I was stunned that she could not see the hand of God in any of it.

When we engaged in spiritual or philosophical discussions, she always resorted to reason and science, which she believed could explain almost all. For what she could not explain, she was comfortable believing that there was no explanation. She never bought that there was a God behind it all. Or in it all. Or over it all. Or in existence, at all. We could have agreed to disagree, but instead I decided to move on.

HANDLING PAPAL AFFAIRS

In the fall of 1998, I fell into an opportunity to return to the radio airwaves when a saint-in-the-making, Pope John Paul II, announced the first-ever papal visit to St. Louis.

A bright, witty, intelligent young man, Ed Martin, approached Tony Holman, the founder of Covenant Network, with the idea for a one-hour radio show to prepare the population for the arrival of the Pontiff. Tony liked the concept, but as Ed had no broadcasting experience, he said, "Why don't you go and see Zip Rzeppa? If you can get Zip to co-host the show with you, we'll do it."

So Ed approached me, we hit it off, and the "Pope in St. Louis: Plans and Preparations Program" was born. It was broadcast from noon to 1pm every Monday for many weeks prior to the arrival of the Pope. We did the show on our lunch break.

If you think this was some stuffy, religious broadcast, you're wrong. Ed is hilarious, and we joked about what the weather might be like when the Pope came in January, the traffic, the parking, the tickets, how to handle throngs of people, and more.

At the same time, I served as chairperson of the Community Affairs Committee for the visit and worked with great people in helping to get everything ready.

When the Pope arrived in St. Louis, he was welcomed by something of a meteorological miracle. The cloistered Sisters of the Holy Spirit, those Pink Sisters, along with the other religious orders were ardently praying for good weather.

Well, the Lord answered *all* the prayers. The normal high in late January is 41 degrees. The day the Pope arrived, it was 54. And the second day of his visit, it was 68!

I was a chaperone for the high school and college students that the Pope invited to a youth rally at St. Louis' 20,000-seat sports arena. My heart, soul, and spirit were filled with joy as I marched in the unseasonably-warm temperatures alongside the exuberant youth for 15 blocks, from the famed Arch to the arena. Songs of praise and prayers of thanksgiving rang out non-stop. My exhilaration knew no bounds.

Inside the arena, we listened to a few speakers as we waited for the Pope. The only speaker I remember was one I will never forget. She was a young nun in full habit. She shared how after college she had entered the business world and rocketed toward the top. She worked night and day and received one promotion after another, until she was hit by a strange feeling of utter emptiness.

She said she thought she was living the American dream. She told us how the Lord came to her and said, "You're *not* living the American dream! You're living the American *nightmare*. I am your dream!" She gave witness to how she quit the business world, entered a cloister, and was filled with the love and the joy and the peace of the Lord every day.

This young woman's beauty could not be hidden under her habit. Her face was radiant as the joy of the Lord emanated from her. It filled the arena.

After the speakers, the jam-packed crowd was led in song by Steve Angrissano and Tom Booth, two great Catholic singer/songwriters. I still remember lyrics that Angrissano wrote expressly for the occasion:

> *"Say not that you are too young, we are holy, we are strong.*
> *In purity and love and faith, the Lord be glorified.*
> *Be holy! The Lord be glorified,*
> *Be holy! Cry the gospel with your life.*
> *We're standing at the gateway of our Faith,*
> *On the rock of Peter and the saints,*
> *With the Holy Spirit showing us the way —*
> *To be holy, and cry the gospel, cry the gospel*
> *With your life."*

We sang that song, and others, until a video feed hit the JumboTron screen. As the Pope's plane, Shepherd One, landed at Lambert International Airport, a thunderous roar rocked the building.

But that was nothing. 40 minutes later, when Pope John Paul entered the arena riding in an open golf cart, the place went nuts. I mean, nuts. The best way I can put it is this: as a TV sportscaster, I have been in countless arenas for NBA Playoff games, the Stanley Cup Playoffs, and NCAA March Madness, and I've seen far more than my share of frenzied sports fans. But I can attest that the decibel level at *none* of those events matched the roar of the crowd when the Pope appeared.

I've witnessed plenty of standing ovations for sports teams and sports stars, but I never witnessed anything like this: the youth continued their ovation as the de facto Popemobile made a number of tours around the arena. The undiminished roar continued as JPII made his way slowly up onto the stage. The noise was deafening as he stood and waved to each side of the crowd. Then he sat down. But the roar did not stop. The Pope stood and motioned for the crowd to be seated. They would have none of it! These young people, almost all of them in the presence of John Paul II for the only time of their life, continued to yell their lungs out.

To say it was the longest ovation I've ever witnessed is a gross understatement. The longest ovation I ever heard at a sports event may have lasted for a couple of minutes. The undiminishing ovation for Pope John Paul II lasted for *eleven* minutes. I know. I timed it. I couldn't believe it. And I'll never forget it.

After the Pope addressed the youth, a young man walked up and presented the Pontiff with a hockey stick. At the arena of the NHL's St. Louis Blues, it was an appropriate gift from a youthful sports enthusiast to an older one. Well, the Pope rose from his seat, looked at the crowd, and made a comical promise he knew he could not keep. "I will come back and play for the Blues," he said. As the crowd roared, he carried the stick to the edge of the stage and pretended to take a wrist shot. From the crowd reaction, you would have thought the Blues had won the Stanley Cup.

Later that week, the Pope celebrated the Holy Sacrifice of the Mass at the Edward Jones Dome before the largest indoor gathering in St. Louis history, more than 104,000 people.

I couldn't resist adding a special papal touch to that week's edition of The Zippo Awards. With assistance from my longtime sports producer, the terrifically talented Mark Halfmann, I decided to make the Pope's "promise" come true.

We took video from a Blues game and doctored it up. When the camera panned the team bench, we superimposed the Pope's face over the face of one of the players. It looked for all the world as if JPII was in uniform for the Blues! We took video of the Blues scoring a couple of goals, and replaced the face of the goal scorers with the face of the Pope. I did a mock play-by-play: "The puck is sent out in front—and the Pope scores!!!!!"

I was wondering if I was going to be criticized by TV station management or the Archbishop or other church officials or the public for irreverence, but no one complained. I was glad. The stunt was my typical out-of-the-box way of honoring a Pope whom I loved, a Pope who loved sports, a Pope who brought so much joy to the people of St. Louis.

When the Pope departed for Rome, our radio show, "The Pope in St. Louis: Plans and Preparations Program" was obsolete. But Tony Holman liked the program so much, he asked Ed Martin and me to come up with something new.

The Holy Father proclaimed a Jubilee year for the millennial year 2000, so we re-named the radio program, "The Jubilee Countdown Show." The next January, when the Jubilee year began, we shortened the title to, "The Jubilee Show." When the Jubilee year ended, we were tired of re-naming the program, so we dubbed it, "Extraordinary Times." We figured that would last for a while. In all, Ed and I did the various versions every Monday for four years. We were honored to do every show as unpaid volunteers, and we had a blast.

HANDS TOGETHER

In case you're wondering how Pope John Paul II decided to visit *St. Louis*, it was through his relationship with Cardinal Justin Rigali. A native of Los Angeles, Rigali worked at the Vatican for 30 years before the Pope appointed him Archbishop of St. Louis in 1994. Less than five years later, Rigali influenced his friend to come to town.

In 2001, Archbishop Rigali called a Eucharistic Congress in St. Louis to "give expression to our faith and our love for our Lord Jesus Christ *truly, really, and substantially present*—body, blood, soul and divinity—in the Sacrament of the Holy Eucharist."

The Congress was held in June on the weekend of the Feast of Corpus Christi.

I was honored to share emcee duties with Auxiliary Bishop Michael Sheridan, who worked with 1,400 volunteers to organize the event. The keynote was delivered by Cardinal Jan Pieter Schotte, Vatican Secretary General of the Synod of Bishops. He recounted how, as a young boy during World War II, he was entrusted to carry The Holy Eucharist to a safe place from his village church, which was about to be destroyed by Allied troops for security purposes.

Other speakers included author and TV host, Father Benedict Groschel, and National Director of *Priests for Life,* Father Frank Pavone. Holy Mass was celebrated at the site of the 1999 Papal Mass, the Edward Jones Dome. Even without the Pope, attendance hit 35,000 people.

My assignment was to welcome the crowd and draw them into a spirit of reverence before Mass. Many times I'd heard the stadium announcer's booming voice over the loudspeakers inciting football fans to make noise, but now here I was, trying to get 35,000 people to *be quiet.*

165

After Mass, many thousands followed Archbishop Rigali as he led a slow and beautiful Eucharistic Procession to the Gateway Arch, the world-class sculpture that extends 630 feet skyward on the banks of the Mississippi. The multitude sat and knelt on the grass under the Arch for Benediction and the Divine Praises. A surge of energy and grace permeated my being as thousands joined voices to sing, *Holy God, We Praise Thy Name.* To further honor the Presence of the Lord, a spectacular fireworks show was launched from a barge on the river.

AN EARLY SALUTE

Less than two years later, I emceed another event at the Edward Jones Dome—the annual St. Louis Mayor's Prayer Breakfast. My TV friend and colleague Larry Conners emceed the annual breakfast for many years, but for some reason I can't recall, Larry had to bow out this time and I was asked to replace him.

The Prayer Breakfast was usually held at a downtown hotel, but this year a much larger venue was needed because of the guest speaker—Kurt Warner. A couple of months earlier, Warner had led the St. Louis Rams to their second Super Bowl appearance in three years.

Fancy dining tables covered the entire playing field. 4,000 people ate breakfast, listened to the mayor, and prayed with ministers from various churches. I took the podium and gave the most famous quarterback in St. Louis history a rousing introduction, which brought the crowd to its feet.

Kurt walked back and forth across the stage, inspiring each soul in the building with his message that football was not as important as his relationship with Jesus Christ. After he received a long standing ovation, I introduced a man from the event's sponsor, an organization called *Christian Business Men for Christ* (CBMC).

This man was on fire with love for the Lord, and asked everyone in attendance, who had not already done so, to say a short prayer, inviting Jesus to come into their hearts. He then asked everyone to fill out one of the small white cards on the tables. There were numerous boxes to check, among them, "I prayed this prayer for the first time today" and "I would like someone from CBMC to follow up for fellowship."

A few days later, I got a call from the CBMC. Pleased with my work, they wanted me to emcee the Prayer Breakfast the following year. Their invitation created a dilemma. On the one hand, the Prayer Breakfast was edifying. Where else could you find four thousand people coming together to pray, and to hear Kurt Warner and other leaders praise the Lord Jesus? But at the same time, I knew the fellowship follow-ups of the CBMC would fail to mention the Sacraments which came to us from Jesus Himself. I desperately want everyone who loves the Lord to be fully aware of His Presence in the Eucharist. It saddened me that so many people could be so alive in Christ, but not recognize Him in His True Presence. I feared that some Catholics might get caught up in the enthusiasm of our dear Christian brothers, and be led away from the Faith.

I turned down the invitation to emcee.

A SHOW OF HANDS

After seven fulfilling years at MERS, I felt moved to use my broadcasting gift full-time. A St. Louis radio station, 1380 AM, was selling blocks of airtime, and I bought the 6am-9am, Monday-through Friday time slot. I figured I could sell enough ads to make a profit.

The GOOD Morning Show, with *GOOD* spelled in capital letters, would present everything good---good quality, good guests, good humor, no objectionable material. I assembled the cast.

Ed Martin magnanimously agreed to co-host, without pay. A very funny young woman, Michele, quit her job at MERS to join us. We dubbed her, "Michele with One L." A young graduate from Boston University ran into me at the Carmelite Novena, saying he wanted to work in radio. He became our board operator. Today, Ben Boyd is the executive sports director at the 50,000-watt giant, KMOX. Declan Duffy and Steve Rupp played major roles, volunteering to appear before they began their work day at MERS.

The show was witty, fast-paced, informative, unpredictable, and exciting, complete with sound effects, plus call-ins from top entertainers and celebrities, including O'Reilly, Costas, and Vitale.

We had two major challenges. The station's weak signal, which reached only about half of St. Louis, and generating ad revenue. I banged on sponsors' doors each day, but they were reluctant to support an unproven product on a weak station.

On a stronger station, we could have made a big splash. As it was, we persisted, and after nine months, we were nearing the break-even point. The future looked pretty good.

Then the station was sold. To a group based in *Utah.* They didn't know me, they didn't care about the show, they were turning the station into an all-sports format. My broadcast friends told them that I could be a big asset. I met with the new manager, and he offered me a job in morning-drive, but in the all-sports format. I begged him to keep *The GOOD Morning Show* instead. He said he'd get back to me.

I was sitting at home on a Friday evening when I got a call from the new boss.

"The show you did this morning—was your last show."

I had been fired in the newspapers in Boston, and now I was being fired over the phone. The world of broadcasting can be brutal.

AN ARTIST'S TOUCH

In need of a job, I crawled back to MERS. Dr. Lew welcomed me back, but as my old position was filled, he sent me to a small auxiliary office. I shared a cubicle with a young woman named Sara. She had produced an array of art, in various forms. A genuine, budding artist. She needed the modest paycheck from MERS to make ends meet.

We worked together in a room the size of a walk-in closet, right next to the unisex restroom. The walls were so thin, we heard every flush. There we were, the ex-broadcaster and the starving artist, crammed together, serving people with mental and/or physical disabilities, changing their lives by helping them find jobs.

Much of our day was spent out in the field, transporting clients to job interviews, or scoping out prospective job sites. But when we were in the office, we talked about art, TV, film, romance, you name it.

A few months later, Sara put on a wonderful multi-art form show. I haven't seen her in years, but I hope she's touching many through her art. Maybe someday she'll be famous, we'll re-connect, and laugh about the days we spent scrunched together next to the latrine.

HOLDING ON TO LIFE

In the autumn of 2001, I went through a seemingly benign procedure to reduce the effects of varicose veins in my feet. A few days after the treatment, I woke up at three in the morning with intense pains in my chest and back. I dialed 9-1-1.

The EMT guys said my pulse and blood pressure were low. They rushed me to the hospital. As a possible heart attack victim, I received immediate attention. After listening to my heartbeat, the doctor said, "Huh, your heartbeat sounds fine."

"Then what's causing these pains, Doc?"

"I don't know. You work out, right? It could be some muscular strain or stress."

I wasn't buying it, but what could I do? They decided to do some tests. They wheeled me into x-ray and when I returned to the ER, suddenly six people in scrubs—doctors, nurses, whoever—were hovering over me.

I asked, "What's going on?"

A doctor responded, "You have multiple blood clots in your left lung, and your right lung, and a clot in the pulmonary artery of your heart. If we had released you, you would have had a 50/50 chance of being dead by this afternoon."

I almost fainted. They pumped blood thinner into my arm and told me not to move. Movement could cause blood clots to flow to the heart or the brain and kill me. They slowly and carefully wheeled me to a hospital room where I spent the next ten days until the clots subsided. Those clots were the closest I had come to death since facing the alleged gunman in Forest Park. The Lord spared me once again.

During my hospital stay, I was faithfully visited by a beautiful woman whom I had dated earlier. Every day she would bring me something new—cookies, treats, books, magazines, culminating with a brand new St. Louis Cardinals jacket. She'd sit with me on her lunch break. Her affection was obvious, but I wasn't really available. I was interested in someone else.

A HAND TO HOLD

I'll call her Natalie. She was a very attractive woman who worked for the state of Missouri. She referred clients to MERS. She had never been married. Declan said she had the most loving heart of any counselor in town. Inspired by that endorsement, I took chase.

When I caught up to her, I was attracted in many ways. She had lived through some tough times and difficult relationships, and I admired her resilience. She was obviously intelligent, and she proved to be a great listener. She served her disabled clients with kindness and consolation. She wasn't a big sports fan, but I figured we could fix that.

I dated Natalie for several months, and then proposed. I was so excited when she said, "Yes." Finally, I had found the one! We went through marriage prep with the same priest who had uncovered the fatal flaw in my previous engagement. I shared with Natalie the pain of that experience. To my relief, the priest found no problems with our test answers.

Our wedding day was set for a Saturday in June of 2002. I was excited beyond words. I was 50 years old, Natalie was ten years younger, and we were both in excellent shape. I was filled with hope that if God willed, we would have a family.

I chose Declan Duffy as my best man. Bill O'Reilly flew in to serve as my groomsman, as I had done for Bill years earlier in New York.

With my groomsman on the day of my wedding

On the morning of my wedding, bright sunshine cascaded down upon the dome of the most beautiful church in America, the Cathedral Basilica of St. Louis. My tuxedoed friends escorted the happy guests to their seats. As the magnificent organ filled the air with the prelude to the rest of my life, Declan, O'Reilly, and I shared a private moment.

Reflecting on the guests, Declan said, "There's quite a few women here who are disappointed right now."

I sucked in a deep breath and slowly exhaled. I felt a surge of certainty and confidence rush through my entire being. I looked at Dec, and I looked at Bill, and said, "I'm sure I'm marrying the right one."

As my bride walked down the aisle, I was almost short of breath. She looked so beautiful! I met her at the step leading to the altar, and her dad gave her away. He looked me in the eye, and said, "Take her— she's yours." My eyes welled up with tears, as I fought hard to hold it together.

Following the readings delivered by two prominent St. Louis newscasters, and Monsignor's stirring homily, it was time for us to exchange vows. It seemed like I had waited my entire adult life for this moment. Finally, it was my turn to enter into a bond with a woman that would last 'till death do us part.

As the Mass progressed, my only regret was that Natalie could not receive the Holy Eucharist, as she was not Catholic. I rejoiced that Natalie, even though she was an agnostic, had embraced the tradition of leaving the altar to present a rose at the feet of the statue of Mary. I remember standing with my bride, imploring the intercession of our Mother on our marriage.

We celebrated at a spectacular reception thrown by Natalie's wonderful dad at the Missouri Botanical Garden on a perfect, 70-degree evening. After a sumptuous feast in a lavishly decorated ballroom, we moved the party outdoors where, surrounded by the fabulous collection of trees and plants that make the Botanical legendary, we danced the night away.

The next day we jetted off to Vancouver, British Columbia to begin the honeymoon I had lovingly and joyfully planned. We biked through Stanley Park, visited the marketplace, floated on the water, walked across the Swinging Bridge up in the mountains, took a cruise to Victoria Island where we walked through the famous Butchart Gardens, and stayed at a private oasis rated the most romantic in

North America. We took a seaplane back to Vancouver Harbor, and enjoyed more nights of fabulous food and drink.

We returned to St. Louis and moved into Natalie's house, appearing to the world to be the perfect couple with the perfect marriage.

It was a mirage.

Suddenly, some things didn't seem quite right. For example, Natalie told me she wore a nicotine patch under her wedding dress. I was so surprised. She had never told me that she smoked. I returned home from work each day excited to see my bride and yet she wasn't reflecting my joy. When I asked her what was wrong, Natalie told me she never really wanted to get married. Totally stunned, I asked her why she went through with it. She said her mother desperately wanted her to marry, and her friends told her I was a great guy, and that she should give it a shot, and if it wasn't going well, to just take off and get a divorce.

All the air went out of me. I could hardly breathe. I thought of the wedding vows. I had heard her say them, but now I feared that she had not meant them.

Over time, Natalie confessed that she did not trust any man.

I said, "Wait a minute. What about the question on the marriage prep test, 'Do you trust your fiancé?'"

She said, "Well, you told me about that other woman. I knew if I answered no, the engagement might be over."

This shook me to my core. I remember walking out of the house, and wandering around the neighborhood, dumbfounded. There was no way I could walk off the shock and hurt of realizing that the woman I loved was not committed to love me forever in return. Finally married, at the age of 50, I was eager to *give* myself fully, completely, to the woman that I loved, for the rest of my life. Was it possible that after all of my searching, after the perfect wedding and honeymoon, I could fail at marriage? I was faced with the horror that I might not be able to fix this.

I went to my spiritual director, told him everything, and asked if we should seek an annulment. He thought for a while, and then advised me to try to hold the marriage together, counseling that it was possible things could turn around through God's grace.

One obstacle was Natalie's agnosticism. Her intelligence and compassion led me to believe that, of course, she would grow in knowledge of, and love for, the Lord. I didn't realize that my zeal to share my faith felt to her like just another guy trying to get his way.

Focusing on my own anguish and emptiness, I wasn't aware of the mutual toxicity in our relationship. To the world we looked like the perfect couple, and I was determined that we could *be* the perfect couple, but there were deep cracks in our relationship that I didn't fully understand.

LETTING GO

One day, Natalie became violently ill with vomiting and diarrhea. About the same time, I was afflicted in the same way. After a couple of days, even in sickness, I felt a strong desire to pray in front of the Lord. I went to our small parish Adoration chapel. After spending time with Jesus, I was on my way to the car. A fire truck was parked along the curb. There didn't seem to be any emergency, so I chatted it up with two firemen. They were there to do a routine check of the parish school. They recognized me from my TV days.

"How are you doing, Zip?"

I groaned, "I must have the flu or something. I'm terribly weak. My wife is very sick, too. By the way, my furnace has been acting up. Do you guys know anyone who fixes furnaces?"

One of the men replied, "Zip, if your furnace is acting up, you could have a gas leak! We better come over right now and take a look!"

They discovered that indeed, gas was seeping out. They ordered us to leave the house and have the entire unit replaced immediately. The furnace installers confirmed the firemen's concern. If we had stayed in the house much longer, we would have died from carbon monoxide poisoning.

Our lungs were once again breathing clean air, but the poison of our problems did not leave with the faulty furnace. In my mind, I was trying to show Natalie how to grow in holiness. But to her, I was polluting the air with my sanctimonious determination to save the marriage by saving her soul.

One beautiful spring morning, Natalie and I were driving around doing errands. I was soaking in the beauty of nature, the new leaves on the trees, the fresh flowers, the green grass. I was keenly aware of the beauty of God's creation, and I voiced praise to the Creator. I was surprised when Natalie took issue with my joy. She said, "I can't take this anymore."

This was the last hour Natalie and I spent together as a couple.

Natalie took off in her car, and she never came back. I never saw her again except for two occasions—the first was eight months later in divorce court. She emailed me the divorce papers from the Internet, and we amicably agreed to split up our assets.

For $225, we obtained a lawyer-free divorce. Later, the Catholic Church granted an annulment, recognizing that our vows were incomplete.

IN THE HANDS OF GOD

The whole relationship and faux marriage left me all but destroyed, emotionally and psychologically. My dreams of a loving family life were shattered. I had to find a way to go on living. What kept me together and sustained me, was Jesus Christ Himself.

I settled into a routine of going to work, eating dinner, heading to a coffee shop where I would do a little writing—writing was therapeutic—and then at nine or ten or eleven o'clock at night, I'd make long visits to Love itself, my Best Friend, my Lord and my God, in His earthly Presence in the Holy Eucharist, in the chapel at my parish.

I would alternately kneel and sit with Him, His Presence in the Host only about four feet away. I would talk to Him, listen, just sit in silence. Always, I received consolation from the God Who knows all, Who knows everything that has happened, Who knows everything about me. The God Who loved me enough to die on the Cross to save me. He reached into my soul and began to heal my interior life.

I certainly didn't know it then, but God had a different bride in mind for me.

I was almost always alone with the Lord during those long nights in the Chapel, but about once a week He sent me a companion. Tim was tall, lean, and middle-aged. In the past year, his son had fallen into addictive drug use, committed a number of crimes, and had been sent to prison. Tim's wife, in trying to cope with the tragedy of their son, and raise their young daughter, had become an alcoholic. Then Tim, a skilled, experienced, job-toughened construction worker, injured his knee and lost his job.

Tim had met Natalie, and, like many others on the outside, assumed we had a solid marriage. My update stunned him. We were a pair of suffering souls, sitting in the Presence of grace and love and mercy. Sometimes Tim would bring his guitar and gently sing songs he had written to the Lord. I had no idea that in the not-too-distant future, Tim and I would be working together.

MANY HANDS, LIGHT WORK

Out of the blue, I got a call from the Board President of the St. Louis Council of the Society of St. Vincent de Paul (SVDP). After much prayer, I accepted the position of executive director of the organization. A big job. The SVDP Council office supported the efforts of 2,600 lay Vincentian volunteers serving the poor, the needy, and the suffering in 140 area parishes as part of an apostolate with a presence in 70 countries around the world.

The SVDP Board charged me with increasing the spirituality of the St. Louis Council. To accomplish this, I hired talented, spiritual *people*, among them, the Irish leprechaun, Declan Duffy, to be Program Director, ten years after *he* had brought *me* to MERS; daily Communicant and financial crackerjack, Mary Kay Leary, to be CFO; Steve Rupp, the luge bowler and a fearless pro-life warrior, to improve relationships with the parishes; and a beautiful, holy young woman, Elizabeth Daub, to handle multiple assignments.

The Lord sent people in all kinds of ways. Tim Massey, an attorney, was volunteering. *He quit his job* to run our utilities program, which helped thousands to keep the lights, heat, and air conditioning on. One day when my car was in the shop, a bright, young man from Enterprise, Ryan Carney, picked me up in a rental. I mentioned my position, and he confided his desire to serve. Two weeks later, he got out of the corporate rat race and came to work at SVDP.

But the most unusual new hire was yet to come. Declan and I sat in my office with a tan, intelligent looking, middle-aged man named Greg. Greg was looking for work. We listened with fascination to his story.

A graduate of Harvard Law School, he had worked for a big-time law firm in Manhattan. He moved to Southern California where he acted in industrial films and served as a "script doctor," re-writing screenplays for Hollywood movies. Then he was introduced to cocaine. He never detailed the extent of his using and dealing, but he was arrested, tried, convicted, and sent to federal prison at Leavenworth.

I don't recall how many years he served, but it was more than a few. And now he sat before us, humbly applying for a job in serving the poor. But that wasn't all.

"I just got married. My wife is the daughter of a Catholic priest."

Our mouths dropped open. Dec and I scratched our heads. "Huh?"

Greg smiled. "Oh, it's all legit. My wife's father was an Anglican priest, legitimately married. He converted to Catholicism, and the Church allows such men to serve as priests while retaining their wife and family."

Dec and I looked at each other. We were sitting with an ex-drug dealer, ex-con, Harvard Law School graduate, son-in-law of a married Catholic priest. *Just another day at St. Vincent de Paul!*

It would have been easy to say goodbye to Greg, to say we'd get back to him, to tell him we had no openings. But that's not where the Holy Spirit led us. We did plenty of due diligence over the next few days, and found nothing to refute any part of Greg's story. We met with him again. In the course of friendly conversation, Greg nonchalantly displayed a vocabulary that would have impressed a genius. For all we knew, he *was* a genius.

So we hired Greg to run a new program called *Good Works*. The purpose was to provide free home repair for seniors who were too poor or too incapacitated to do the work themselves. Greg did such a great job we needed to hire a construction expert to expand and run the program.

I knew where to find one. My Adoration Chapel companion, Tim!

Tim rolled into the position full of steam. The housing market had collapsed, so Tim recruited out-of-work or laid-off construction folks, and over the next two years, they repaired more than *1,000 homes* in the metro area.

As I write this, Tim's son remains incarcerated, but his wife hasn't had a drink in years. In June of 2014, I had the honor and privilege of celebrating with her as Tim was ordained a Deacon in the Roman Catholic Church. God works in marvelous ways.

As for Greg, we moved him to head up another new program— *Vinnie's Autos.*

Historically, SVDP took in donated cars and generated revenue by selling the parts, tires, etc. Declan and I wondered, why not get these cars to the poor who need them to get to work?

Greg used his brilliance—and newfound desire to serve—to form 54 strategic partnerships with Vincentian volunteers, towing companies, repair shops, and detailers, who slashed their rates to make our donated cars road worthy.

Greg offered the poor a deal they couldn't refuse—a reliable car to get them to work— no money down, $80 per month for 12 months. And if someone couldn't make a payment or two, he wouldn't swoop in and re-possess the car, and ruin their credit for life. No, he'd *forgive the debt!*

Greg applied Catholic social teaching in affirming the importance of all. The car buyers had the dignity of paying for their wheels, and their payments allowed us to continue to fix cars for others.

More than 350 people in need are driving cars because of Greg's ingenuity. A Harvard Law school grad can do amazing things in the hands of God!

THROWING A GOOD PITCH

As we grew SVDP's programs and services, we needed to increase funding. I found an unexpected resource from *Hollywood*. O'Reilly invited Steve McEveety on our 2006 Men of Adventure trip to Nassau. Steve had been either the producer or executive producer of virtually every major movie starring Mel Gibson—*The Passion of the Christ, Braveheart, We Were Soldiers, What Women Want, Lethal Weapon I and II and III and IV,* and the rest.

Steve and I hit it off. I told him about the poor and the needy that we served, and Steve readily agreed to appear in St. Louis. We billed the event, *An Evening with Steve McEveety, Producer of The Passion of the Christ.*

A capacity crowd of 250 potential donors packed the elegant 40th floor downtown restaurant, Kemoll's. Kemoll's owner, Mark Cusumano, donated everything—the dinner, the space, the waiters, the booze. Steve captivated the guests with a dramatic account of the making of *The Passion*--- how he slept with a large crucifix on his chest every night, how *two* lightning strikes hit the same crew member who not only survived, but later had his baby baptized by Pope John Paul II, how he carried a copy of *The Passion* to Rome and got it into the hands of the Pope, and how the Pontiff's comment, "It is as it was," helped promote the picture in the face of intense negative media publicity.

After Steve's dramatic presentation, I told the guests that SVDP needed their help to serve the poor, the needy and the suffering. They responded by donating more than $200,000.

McEveety had another reason to be in St. Louis. He met with people who opposed an amendment to allow embryonic stem cell research in Missouri.

The embryonic research, which could lead to human cloning, was supported by universities positioned to receive hundreds of millions in research money. Their allies included many scientists and major medical interests. Their coalition had a ton of money, and they pushed a cleverly worded proposal onto the ballot. Planting positive stories in the media, the cloners' side built up a seemingly insurmountable 65% to 35% lead in a poll done just six weeks before the election.

That's when those on the side of protecting human life powerfully swung into action. Cardinal Raymond Burke, at the time Archbishop of St. Louis, urged all parish priests to tell the faithful that while the Church supported *adult* stem cell research which could lead to medical cures, it opposed *embryonic* stem cell research, as it destroyed the life of human embryos. Many churches and synagogues joined in to oppose Amendment 2.

McEveety struck a mighty blow. He produced a 30-second TV spot in which celebrities urged voters to "Vote No on 2." The celebrities included Kurt Warner; Kansas City Royals all-star first baseman Mike Sweeney; actress Patricia Heaton, who played the beloved wife on *Everyone Loves Raymond*; and popular St. Louis Cardinals starting pitcher, Jeff Suppan.

My great friend, Catholic radio host, speaker, and author Deby Schlapprizzi, found an anonymous donor who contributed $125,000 to help us flood the airwaves with the TV spot.

As Election Day neared, Suppan pitched the Cardinals into the World Series. He was the winning pitcher against the Mets in the deciding Game 7 of the National League Championship Series, and was named the NLCS Most Valuable Player.

Then, with the election a week away and the Cardinals leading the American League champion Tigers 2-1 in games, Suppan was to pitch Game 4 of the World Series.

On the day of his start, the top story in the St. Louis Post-Dispatch was about how Suppan was appearing in the TV spot opposing Amendment 2. Cardinals fans who supported Amendment 2, apparently more interested in the World Series than in protecting human life, stormed the media, lashing out at Suppan. Not only did they oppose Jeff's position on the research, they felt he should be concentrating on pitching instead of making a TV pitch.

Reality set in. If Suppan lost Game 4, and the Cardinals went on to lose the World Series in the days before the election, countless disgruntled fans may be motivated to go to the polls and vote for cloning.

McEveety flew back to California. He rarely watched baseball, but was glued to the TV screen and praying for Suppan between *every pitch*. I was at the game with Deby Schlapprizzi and her husband, Don. We cheered out hearts out as Suppan, under tremendous pressure, pitched courageously. He kept the Cardinals in the game, and after he was relieved, the Cards went on to win. The very next night, they won again to wrap up the World Series title. Perhaps now people might be motivated to come out and vote *with* Suppan!

On election day, Deby and I went on local radio stations and urged voters to "Vote No on 2."

Early in the evening, as the polls were about to close, I was kneeling in a chapel in front of the Lord Jesus, praying with Jason Jones. Jason was a powerful force in getting out the pro-life vote in state and national elections. He moved to St. Louis for a couple of months to organize our ground fight.

Jason has lived an amazing life. At 17, he got his girlfriend pregnant. He was preparing to care for her and the baby when she told him that her father had forced her to get an abortion. He told her he would prosecute her father for murder. She told him that since the Roe vs. Wade decision in 1973, the killing of their baby was legal in the United States.

Stunned and flabbergasted, Jason decided to devote the rest of his life to fighting for the protection of unborn children. He has used his tall, powerful presence, compelling speaking voice, emotional witness, heartfelt passion, and dogged determination to bring the message of life to countless people around the world.

He has dug wells for the starving in the Sudan, produced the award-winning short film, Crescendo, about how the abortion of Beethoven was averted, and established Movies to Movement to steer people to wholesome, moral films.

A couple of weeks before the election, Jason and I "educated" voters outside the gates of the St. Louis vs. Kansas City NFL game. On their way in, hundreds of fans got a passionate earful from Jason and me about the evils of human cloning.

On election night, we sat exhausted in the "Vote No on 2" election headquarters. Most of our opponents had packed it in at their site, where they had planned a jubilant celebration. But their celebration never happened. Well past midnight, their once-certain victory had turned into an election too close to call.

The next morning, the cloners won, but the margin was so slim, pro-life forces immediately announced plans to put a more favorably worded issue on the next ballot, and, with more time to rally, they vowed to defeat embryonic research and cloning efforts. Since the research would cost hundreds of millions of dollars and many years to implement, the cloning forces folded, and decided not to bring embryonic research into Missouri. A great de facto victory, against steep odds, for life!

A GENTLE TOUCH

We continued to meet unmet needs at SVDP. We created the *Medical Transportation Program* to get people to and from their medical procedures. Kevin Corrigan, a devout Catholic, was the perfect person to launch it.

When our lay volunteers identified people who needed chemotherapy, radiation, and other medical procedures and could not drive, we sent Kevin to transport them. In the Spirit of the Lord, he did much more than that. After driving the diseased to the treatment center, Kevin remained with them, often sitting by their side while an IV dripped into their arm for hours. He shared in their struggle—the despair, the uncertainty, the suffering of their often terminal illnesses. He was Christ to them, providing companionship, comfort, strength and support. On the return drive home, Kevin provided hope and a different kind of healing, praying with them in their Gethsemane.

A HAND UP

We addressed the homeless problem. Herding the homeless into barracks-like facilities wasn't working. Duh! So we hired Gretchen Shipp and Joe Piskulic, two terrific social workers with a new idea. *Project More.* It became a huge success.

The concept was to help the homeless into safe apartments *first,* and then, when they weren't freezing or sweating to death, we'd address the addictions and illnesses and unemployment that contributed to their plight.

A perfect example was Melvin. He had diabetes, high blood pressure, and was schizophrenic. He hated homeless shelters. He told us, "You have to sleep with one eye open, because you can't trust anybody." Not a nice way to live. Joe found Melvin sleeping behind a dumpster.

Joe befriended him, and brought him to a clean, vacant apartment. After living for several years on the streets, Melvin was certainly out of his comfort zone.

"You mean, I can stay here?"

"No, Melvin," Joe replied. "You can *live* here. This is your place."

"Wow. It's got heat."

"Yep, and a bathroom. And a kitchen. And here's your bedroom."

"Great! I'll put my sleeping bag right here."

"You're not going to need your sleeping bag, Melvin. Wait till you see what we've got for you.

Out to the street, SVDP volunteer George was arriving with a full pick-up truck.

Melvin was incredulous. "You mean, I can use this stuff?"

Joe smiled. "Melvin, you can *keep* this stuff. It's yours. All you have to do is take care of it."

Melvin enthusiastically helped Joe and George move a bed, a couch, a chair, and a TV set into the apartment, along with sheets, towels, and dishes.

Melvin's case was off to a good start, but just beginning. SVDP would pay Melvin's rent for three months. He would be expected to pay 25% of the rent for the next three months, then 50% for the three months after that, and at the one-year mark, the goal was for Melvin to be totally self-sustaining.

Joe got him the vital medical and psychiatric help he desperately needed, and when his health improved, Joe helped him find a job.

A year later, Melvin hardly recognized himself. Each day, he would shave and shower and arrive to work on time. He paid his bills, and became good friends with his neighbors. We were so inspired by Melvin's turnaround, we wanted to share his story.

We got a production company to shoot and produce a video, pro bono. It wasn't exactly *Lifestyles of the Rich and Famous*. Small apartment. Cheap furniture. Simple job. And yet, Melvin was a *huge* success. He had defeated homelessness, mental illness, unemployment, and the hope-less-ness of life on the streets.

Little did I sense that the video of Melvin would help us raise half a million dollars.

PULLING IT IN

As we served more people, we needed more funding. I reached out to O'Reilly. He agreed to come into St. Louis and headline a gala fundraiser. The date was set for a Friday in September. It turned into much more of an ordeal than anyone imagined.

It was the election year of 2008. The week before our event, Bill did *The O'Reilly Factor* in Denver from the Democratic National Convention. The week *of* our event, he did *The Factor* from the Republican National Convention in Minneapolis. He was to return to New York to do the show on Thursday, and then fly to St. Louis for our fundraiser on Friday.

Barack Obama inadvertently altered the plans.

Obama suddenly agreed to do the interview that all *Factor* fans were hungering for, *if* O'Reilly would meet him on the campaign trail in Easton, Pennsylvania *the next day*. On Thursday, Bill flew from Minneapolis to Easton, did the most powerful interview of the campaign, flew to New York, anchored the *The Factor*, went home, slept, re-packed, got up before dawn, and headed to a small airport on Long Island.

Missouri businessman, L.B. Eckelkamp, sent his jet to fly him to St. Louis. The moment he landed, we drove to the Drury Hotel for Bill's live, two-hour broadcast of *The Radio Factor*. Charles Drury brought in his top chef to prepare a lunch. We drove 25 miles to downtown where Bill taped the TV show, then 30 miles to the site of the fundraiser. I do not know how Bill was still standing, but he stood and greeted each guest as if it was the first thing he had done all day.

The renowned Irish tenor, Mark Forrest, launched the event with a stirring rendition of "The Star Spangled Banner." Acclaimed pianist John-Paul Kaplan came in from Chicago and serenaded us all. I introduced Bill. He wowed everyone with a dynamic 20-minute commentary on the election, and then amused one and all in answering endless questions submitted by the guests. I informed the crowd how SVDP serves the poor, and of our need for financial support.

Then we showed the video of "Melvin." People were in tears.

O'Reilly grabbed the microphone and addressed the guests. "Hey, if *you* don't step up to help people like Melvin, *who's going to do it?*"

In the next five minutes, we collected close to $500,000. Bill and Melvin made a heckuva combination.

TOUCHING THE SKY

In 2009, I went on a pilgrimage to Medjugorje in Bosnia-Herze-govina. I wanted to see the place where the Mother of God report-edly began appearing daily to six young people in 1981, and allegedly continues to appear to three of them today.

I made the journey with 27 pilgrims—among them, a fine, devout priest, Father Ed Schramm; a holy, prayerful woman, Judy Brown; SVDP finance director, Mary Kay Leary; and Larry Rice who runs the New Life Evangelistic Center. The others I met for the first time, including my assigned roommate, Michael.

Michael was in his mid-twenties, and full of energy. He had returned to the Faith after turning away for a few years. He was deter-mined to live a holy life, despite the many temptations of the world.

We flew from St. Louis to Detroit to Paris to Croatia, and then took a two-and-a-half hour bus ride up the Adriatic coast. Total travel time was 18 hours. It was 108 degrees when we arrived. We were told that we were blessed. It had been 115 the day before.

We lodged with two local families, half of us in one house enlarged to accommodate pilgrims, and the others in a second, similar home. At dinner, we chatted with our guide, Drago, a friendly, devout Cath-olic, and a big fan of the NBA. Satellite TV has shrunk the world. Here I was, desiring to grow closer to the Lord, and our guide starts talking about European hoop stars and their chances to make the Lakers.

It was close to midnight when we got to bed. The room I shared with Michael had two cots, separated by an "aisle" about 18 inches wide. The bathroom was down the hall. Young Michael could not get to sleep. I understood his challenge. He was about 6-foot-2, and the cots were 6-foot-nothing. The un-air-conditioned room temperature was about 95.

Michael moaned and turned and thrashed about, almost non-stop. Exhausted from the journey, I fell in and out of sleep. Then I heard Michael exclaim, "Wow, it's only three o'clock in the morning."

I was inspired with an idea. I sat up. "Michael, would you like to say The Divine Mercy Chaplet?"

"Sure," he said. "Might as well."

We began with the Sign of the Cross. One Our Father. One Hail Mary. The Apostles' Creed. In the stifling heat, I took the lead. "Eternal Father, I offer you the Body and Blood, Soul and Divinity, of Your dearly beloved Son, Our Lord Jesus Christ…"

Michael responded, "…in atonement for our sins, and those of the whole world."

We grabbed our rosaries, and repeated this short prayer on each of the 50 small beads.

We prayed the concluding prayers in unison.

"Holy God, Holy Mighty One, Holy Immortal One, have mercy on us and on the whole world."

"Jesus, I trust in You."

In the next three minutes, Michael fell into a deep sleep. It took quite an effort to wake him up for breakfast.

We spent the next four days walking narrow streets lined with shops selling rosaries, crucifixes, and other devotional articles. Almost all of the town's residents attend daily Mass, and many spend three hours per day in prayer. We joined them at their one and only parish church, St. James. Drago the Guide said that when the church was renovated decades earlier, the parish priest was inspired to enlarge it to accommodate 1,000 people, even though the *total* population of the village's five hamlets had never exceeded 400. Somehow he knew a bigger church would be needed. And then some. Today, an exterior extension accommodates an additional 5,000.

We were among the 40 million visitors who have journeyed to the little, out-of-the-way village. I did not receive a visit from the Blessed Mother, nor did I anticipate one. That wasn't why I made the long trip. I was seeking to grow closer to the Lord and His Mother, and on the afternoon of the third day, they blessed us with a miracle.

I was with Michael and seven other members of our group at the base of a mountain. It was about 3:30, with the summer sun high in the sky. I don't recall the instant it began, but we almost simultaneously found ourselves staring at the sun. *Staring!* No one can stare directly at the sun without damaging their eyes, *but that's what we were doing.* We marveled to each other that it was no more difficult to stare into the sun than it was to look at a cloud. But there were no clouds. It was a cloudless sky.

The sun appeared to contain a white object which all but filled its circumference. Someone in our group exclaimed, "It's like the Body of Christ!" an obvious reference to the Lord in the Holy Eucharist.

Before long, a trail of something—a meteor, a cloud, some substance—appeared to extend out from the right side of the sun. The air was punctuated by our reactions: "Wow." "Whoa." "Look at that." Then Michael's voice rose above the rest.

"It's the Blood of the Lord!"

And since it was reddish in color, it was easy for us to recognize a symbol of the Lord's Blood flowing from the appearance of the Host contained in the sun. We stared at the image for perhaps another 10 minutes, until we could wait no longer to run into the village and share the experience with the rest of our group.

Drago told us that many, many pilgrims had witnessed "miracles of the sun" at Medjugorje, and that more than a few had burned their eyes, hoping and failing to see what we had seen.

FEELING THE HEALING

On the fourth and final day of our visit, I witnessed a "miracle" of a completely different sort. About 100 feet to the left of the entrance to St. James Church, there was a wall with 25 doors, each spaced about six feet apart. It was part of a structure about 150 feet in length, but only 10 feet in width. It was open air—no roof. It was the largest and strangest *confessional* I had ever seen!

Each of the 25 doors was marked by the language in which confessions were heard. The penitents lined up. Some lines had one or two people, other lines ran 10 to 12 deep, determined by the native tongue of the confessors. I stared at the people from various parts of the world, some of them in tears, preparing to receive the forgiveness of the Lord.

I was aware of the words of Jesus to His apostles after His Resurrection: "Receive the Holy Spirit. Whose sins you shall forgive, they are forgiven them."

Here I stood in close proximity to 25 successors of the Apostles, these holy priests who collectively spoke more than a dozen languages, through whom Jesus Christ was remitting sins and bringing souls back into a state of grace. No wonder tears were flowing!

I prepared my heart to confess my sins. Surrounded by people from so many countries, I was acutely aware of my lowliness. I breathed a prayer.

"Lord God, you existed before all things. You made the earth and all the planets and all the galaxies and the sun and the moon and the stars and the oceans and the continents and all that is in them—the animals and the fish and the trees and the flowers and the plants and the grass—and all the billions of people who have ever lived. How could You, the Creator of everything, look at me, a woeful, totally insignificant little sinner, and decide to send Your only Son to become a human to save *me?"*

I looked around and it hit me. This mercy wasn't just for me.

Since I had left TV, I had come to see Christ in the struggling minds and bodies of the disabled, the homeless, and the homebound. Now I was standing with the Hungarian grandma, the Asian tourist, the Hispanic family, the Pakistani businessman, the Ethiopian mystic, united in the incomprehensible mercy of God.

After my confession, I went into the church to pray my penance. In my prayers of thanksgiving, I marveled at the humility of God.

When the Lord came to save us, He could have come to earth as a great warrior or king or superhero. But instead He came as a tiny embryo. He remained captive in His Mother's womb for nine months! He could have been born in a castle, but instead He was born alongside animals in a shelter.

He spent thirty years in *ordinary life* in a small town in Galilee. He was so unassuming that when he worked a miracle, people were incredulous. "Isn't this the carpenter's son?"

He allowed mere mortals to condemn Him to death. He suffered worse than anyone has ever suffered, and worse than anyone ever will. He gave up his Body and poured out his Blood and died on the Cross so that our sins would not separate us from Him forever.

There in the presence of the Lord, thousands of miles from my home, I was keenly aware that the Lord of Life promises *all of us* a place with Him in his unimaginable Kingdom, where all suffering and sickness and death will be no more. Kneeling in church with dozens of pilgrims whose tongues I did not understand, I was one with them in Christ, rejoicing here on earth

In the mountains of Medjugorje, God awakened me to a faith without boundaries.

Kneeling upright in the white t-shirt on Apparition Hill in Medjugorje

A DIRECTOR'S TOUCH

Returning to SVDP, I sought to inspire more people to become Vincentians—not priests, but lay people willing to serve the poor and needy in their parishes.

Once again, unexpected help arrived from Hollywood.

I got a call from Jason Jones. He was promoting a movie entitled, *Bella.* He put me on the phone with the producer, Leo Severino.

"I made this movie with my two Amigos."

"Uh-huh."

"So we're the three Amigos."

Was that supposed to be a punch line?

"One of the Amigos is Eduardo Verastegui."

"Ok, Leo. Don't know him."

"If you were Hispanic, you would. Here's a snapshot. He was the lead singer of an insanely popular Hispanic boy band, toured in 13 Spanish-speaking countries, then became a heartthrob on the *novellas.*"

"What's a *novella?*"

"A Spanish soap opera. Produced in Mexico. They're seen in all of the Hispanic countries."

"Okay."

"Then Eduardo went to Hollywood. He starred as a womanizer in a sleazy movie, and then, through God's grace, saw the light, repented, and returned to his Catholic Faith."

"Wow."

Leo told me about the other Amigo, Alejandro Monteverde, how he came to the U.S. without knowing a word of English and got into the renowned film school at the University of Texas. He won more film awards than any student in UT history.

As for Leo, he was an attorney at 20ᵗʰ Century Fox, then a programming exec. He quit when the programming went sleazy. He met Eduardo and Alejandro, and formed Metanoia Films to make extraordinary, inspirational movies.

"And *Bella* is your movie?" I asked.

"Yep. Our first one."

Two weeks later, I was the only male sitting in the giant ballroom of a St. Louis hotel with 400 women, watching a private screening of *Bella*. It was terrific. It brought most of the women—and *me*— to tears.

When the lights came up, Leo handed the microphone to an attractive lady. She said, "I loved it. My husband and I will do everything we can to support this film." The woman's husband is Albert Pujols.

After Leo dismissed the women, he told me how the Amigos produced *Bella* on a scant $3 million budget, how Steve McEveety got it into the Toronto Film Festival, and how it won the People's Choice Award over movies with superstar actors and $100 million budgets.

"But we need your help, Zip."

He told me how the movie, with its powerful but non-preachy pro-life ending, had been rejected by the major movie distributors.

"As the winner of the Toronto Film Festival, we should be in 3,000 theaters nationwide, but we're only in about 200. We've got to get people out to see the movie, so we can keep the theaters that we have, and add more."

So I came up with a wild idea to support the film *and* help SVDP to grow. The movie was opening in six St. Louis theaters. I had the SVDP Board buy *$38,000 worth of tickets to Bella*. I *gave* the tickets to our 2,600 volunteers to sell. They kept half of the money to serve the poor in their parishes, and sent the other half to the Council. As they were selling the tickets, they encouraged people to become Vincentians.

The Vincentians came through! The number of Vincentians grew! The weekend the movie opened, I got a call from Leo in Hollywood.

"Hey, have you ever heard of a theater named, *Ronnie's?*"

"Sure. It's right here in St. Louis. Why?"

"Well, the top two grossing theaters for *Bella* were in New York City, which we expected, but the third-highest grossing theater in the country was *Ronnie's.*"

I figured it out. Many of the Vincentians near *Ronnie's* were seniors, so they sold a lot of tickets *to* seniors. Seniors like to go to the movies in daytime. Thus, all the *matinee* showings at *Ronnie's* were jam-packed, and that rocketed *Ronnie's* toward the top.

The other St. Louis theaters drew well, too. Flying against the culture, with little money to promote, the film reached 475 screens. It deserved 3,000.

Saddened that *Bella* didn't get a fair shake, I came up with another idea to help the film *and* SVDP. I approached a dynamo named Suzie Spence, who loved the film as much as I did. She and her husband, Dave, agreed to chair a *Bella* event at the Chase Park Plaza Hotel. To stoke the fire, Suzie and Dave invited influential Catholics to meet the filmmakers at three private screenings in their magnificent home.

The Amigos agreed to fly in for the soirees. It isn't often that a movie star and a movie director and a movie producer are seen in St. Louis, much less *multiple times.*

The event at the Chase was a sellout, the donors loved the film, the Amigos wowed them on stage, and SVDP took in a heck of a lot of money to serve the poor. Through our efforts and those of many others, the Three Amigos have heard from more than 1,000 women who, after seeing *Bella,* chose life for their baby.

My bond grew with the Amigos, amazingly talented men who aim to create major movies that write the Gospel on the hearts and minds of millions, without being preachy. They are striving to produce the prequel to *The Passion of the Christ*, and I'm hopeful that it will rock the world.

HOLDING A WINNING TICKET

An axiom of the great, 17th century saint, St. Vincent de Paul, was to do "More, More, More" to help those in need. So we initiated a pharmacy program for those who could not afford their medications. We re-connected the electricity for those who had been cut off. We offered free sandwiches and bottled water to every destitute person who came through our doors.

Once again needing to increase funding, Declan and I came up with a wacky idea for a giant raffle. We ran it by the president of SVDP's Board, Ron Guz.

Ron served as a Vincentian for many years during his career as an investment banker. He was accustomed to our imaginative fund-raising ideas, but was skeptical of this one.

"A *raffle?* What's next, Bingo?"

"Ron, we'll call it the *Meet Me in Manhattan* raffle."

"We're in St. Louis."

"Exactly! The raffle winner will get a trip for four to *New York*."

"That's it?"

"Uh, no. People can go to New York on their own, but they can't *buy* a visit to watch Bill O'Reilly do *The O'Reilly Factor*."

"Bill would let them do that?"

"Think I can convince him."

"Okay, some people would pay a lot of money for *that*. What else?"

"Well, we can throw in tickets to a Yankees game. And a Broadway show. Give them a chauffeur to drive them around in a limo. And how about $3,000 spending money?"

"Hmmm. I think *I'd* buy a ticket. How much would tickets cost?"

"A hundred bucks. It'll be like *Bella!* The Vincentians will sell the tickets after the Masses, and keep 50 bucks for their parishes."

"I get it. And they can recruit more Vincentians."

"Yup."

After Ron approved, the Holy Spirit elevated the prizes. A native St. Louis chef who made it big in New York, offered dinner plus a kitchen tour of his hot dining spot, BoBo. A generous St. Louisan, Niall Gannon, arranged for a three-night stay at the famed Essex House, the residence of numerous movie stars.

O'Reilly mentioned the raffle on *The Factor*. So many viewers flooded our website that the server blew. When we got the server back up, ticket sales rocketed.

The mayor and other dignitaries came to SVDP for the *Meet Me in Manhattan* drawing. We live-streamed the event over the Internet. The winner was a St. Louis social worker and her husband who, with another couple, took an unforgettable bite out of the Big Apple.

The raffle netted SVDP $125,000 to help us serve the poor.

Ron and the Board continued to put up with our crazy schemes, and the Spirit bestowed blessings in abundance. Within five years, SVDP grew from 2,600 volunteers to more than 3,100. The staff doubled in size, programs almost tripled, two aging thrift stores were closed and four new ones opened. The annual budget went from $2.2 million to $6 million, and awareness of the Society increased exponentially.

Spiritual renewal was also evident. Juraj was a stocky, native Slovakian who learned to speak English by praying the rosary while he drove a cab. We got him out of the taxi and into building maintenance, where he saved us a ton of money because he could build or fix anything.

We assigned Juraj to convert an upstairs room into a chapel. The project was the joy of his heart. He stayed up all night to paint the wall behind the tabernacle in radiant fashion. Thereafter, a priest came in once a week to say Mass for the staff. Led by Juraj in his beautiful, fractured English, the prayers of the rosary echoed off the chapel walls every day.

IN THE MASTER'S HANDS

God had worked in powerful ways through Declan and me and our staff, but now He had other plans for the leprechaun. Dec developed shortness of breath, and the cause of it shocked us all. He was diagnosed with Stage 4 bladder cancer.

He underwent major surgery. Unfortunately, he contracted a staph infection, so chemotherapy and radiation treatments were ruled out. His prognosis was terminal.

Declan had been there before, in the hospice for the dying in Ireland, before his miraculous healing. He simply proclaimed, "God's Will be done."

I visited him in the hospital many a night. He suffered greatly. But when asked about the pain, he would say, "I'm offering it up for my beloved poor." Dec knew he was dying, but in his inimitable spirit, he miraculously pulled off one last hurrah.

He was the lead guitarist and vocalist for a very popular Irish band, the Irish Xiles. The other Xiles were his three sons. Dec formed the band the day after his middle son was released from jail following some drinking and drug issues. It was a clever father's ingenious way of keeping the wayward son out of trouble every Friday and Saturday night.

Due to his illness, Dec had not performed with the Xiles for months. One night in the hospital, he whispered that he was going to play one last gig with his boys, on St. Patrick's Day. I didn't know how to respond. St. Pat's was only a couple of weeks away. I looked at him curled up in his bed, tubes hanging from his arm, a colostomy bag attached to his midsection, and thought, *there's no way.*

Well, I was among several hundred revelers at the Dubliner on bustling Washington Avenue on March 17th, 2011, when they wheeled Declan into the building. His sons and a hot fiddle player were ready to perform. They lifted Dec onto the stage, his colostomy bag concealed in a handsome, leather man-bag hanging from his shoulder. He sat down and grabbed his favorite guitar. I could not believe what I was seeing.

Dec led the band in a super-fast Irish tune, singing with gusto, his Irish accent echoing off the walls. The place went crazy. I was hoping he would play a slow song, just to conserve his energy, but he whipped through two more fast ones before he softened the pace. He and the boys played for an hour with Dec chatting between songs as if he had never been away. His sons in the band, and his fans in the crowd, told me it was the finest set the Irish Xiles ever played.

I ran up to help Dec get back into his wheelchair. Along with his wife and a few close friends, we left the frenzy of the Dubliner, and wheeled our man outside. A young priest and Irish Xiles superfan,

Father Sean, gathered us in prayer on the sidewalk. We reached out to touch our hero as Father Sean said, "All hands on Dec!" Tears flowed as we laughed at the pun, and then we prayed in thanksgiving for the miracle we had just seen. We prayed for another one, for the miraculous healing of Dec, if it was the Father's Will.

But alas, it wasn't. Less than three months later, Dec passed on to his eternal reward at the age of 58. I eulogized my best friend before a huge gathering, following his Memorial Mass. I poured out my heart. I recalled for the mourners how long ago, Dec had confessed to me his addictive personality and how he decided to become addicted to *love*. He went to libraries and book stores and read all he could find about all the *kinds* of love— agapé, eros, puppy, everything. He studied the saints who lived *lives* of love. And his life became a life of love.

With the amazing Declan Duffy after the miracle
on St. Patrick's Day

I spoke for more than an hour. I don't remember how I ended it, but when I finished, everyone was on their feet, laughing and crying and applauding. I invited others to come up and share, but no one came forward. Then someone said, "Let's eat," and as desserts were gobbled and libations consumed, amazing, heartwarming memories of Declan's life were exchanged by all. Dec and his kin in the next world were no doubt smiling down on this wonderful Irish wake.

THE HAND OF GOD

SVDP swirled into a time of transition. Without Declan, and with a new board president coming in, I sensed that God was leading me elsewhere.

I went on an ACTS Retreat. ACTS stands for Adoration, Community, Theology, and Service. The retreat ran for four days and three nights with a group of 50 men. One of the guys was on the Board of Angels' Arms, and he told me the agency was looking for a managing director. I subsequently felt the call, and I stepped aside at SVDP to take the position.

The Angels' Arms mission is all about helping foster children. 75% of the foster children in Missouri, at one point or another, are separated from their siblings. These kids had lost their parents, their school, their neighborhood, their friends, even their pets. And now they were going to lose the last thing they had, their own brothers and sisters?

So a determined mother/teacher founded Angels' Arms. She formed a board, recruited donors, and raised enough money to establish a foster home—a home in a safe neighborhood, in a good school district, with a big backyard where the foster children could play.

A home big enough to house six foster kids and two foster parents. The carefully recruited parents paid just $1.00 per year as rent. With reduced financial pressures, they could be there for the six foster kids, who often came from two or three families.

The first Angels' Arms home was established in 2003. When I arrived in 2011, there were six homes. I looked for ways to further expand. I came across state tax credits available to not-for-profits for the purpose of real estate. I thought, "Bingo! *Real estate?* We qualify." The credits provided donors with a 50% *state tax credit.*

In July, I applied with the state for $500,000 in credits. The waiting process dragged on. The biggest donations come at the end of the tax year, and the time for using the credits was running out.

On December 12th, *the Feast of Our Lady of Guadalupe,* the state tax credits came through! With only 19 days left in the year, I had to find donors with so much revenue they could benefit from knocking 50% of their donation off their *state* taxes.

I prayed to Our Lady of Guadalupe to bring the right people. Two days before Christmas, a super successful yet very humble businessman sent me a check for $500,000. A miracle!

Stunned and overjoyed, I gave thanks to Our Lady of Guadalupe for her intercession! This was hard to believe! With eight days left in the year, I asked Our Lady to continue to help her children. I contacted the state. They granted Angels' Arms another $200,000 in credits.

Four days before the end of the year, I opened an envelope sent in by a devout and holy man whom I had told about our foster kids. I found two checks. One was from the man's business for $100,000, the other was his personal check for another $100,000.

Those without faith had trouble believing it. Our Lady of Guadalupe had brought us the tax credits, and then brought forth two donors who gave Angels' Arms $700,000! We used the money to purchase three sizable houses in good neighborhoods, make all the necessary repairs, and turn them into very special foster homes, homes that provide housing and excellent foster parenting for six foster children per house, 24/7, every day of the year. God willing, they will continue to do so for *hundreds* of foster children over the decades to come.

Fired up and filled with fervor, I moved my 3 x 4-foot image of Our Lady of Guadalupe into my office. I had faith that Our Lady would bring about further miracles to help her children in need.

But the founder/executive director did not share the faith. She called me in, and said that Angels' Arms was not a religious organization, and ordered me to remove Our Lady's image from the building.

I was startled. Referring to Our Lady, I said, "But she's the reason we're getting these three new homes." The director didn't see it that way.

"Zip, you gotta be kidding me. *You* are the reason this money came in."

My mouth dropped open. I knew I didn't have that kind of power! But how could I explain it? It was a miracle. I had called upon Our Lady and she delivered *$700,000* in fifteen days.

"Zip, I'm the boss. You gotta get that painting out of here."

In that moment, I realized I wanted to work for a different woman.

I transported Our Lady's image back to my apartment, and hung her back up on the wall. I looked at the image, and spoke to my Mother. "Our Lady of Guadalupe, I want to work for you."

REACHING UP

A MOTHER'S HANDS

Within days, I was inspired by an idea: Use my gifts in *communications* for the greater glory of God! I took stock of my talents. I had a degree in journalism from Boston University. I had written approximately 8,000 television sportscasts, plus dozens of TV specials. The vision began to crystallize. *Write in a new direction! Books! Books in a fresh voice that could evangelize the Catholic Faith.*

Hundreds of millions of young people were reading *Harry Potter, Twilight, Divergent, The Hunger Games.* Would they read a new genre of *Catholic* novels? And new *biographies* could inspire. Why not create a whole new approach to Catholic *publishing?* Why not write, design, and print dynamic *new books?* To people who couldn't afford to buy them, we'd give them the books for *free.* And why not give *everyone* books for free?

It was a daring idea—but it was totally *crazy.* Was I losing it?

I wasn't sure. But if this was the call, I was going to need a lot of help. Fortunately, I'm a guy who isn't afraid to ask for directions. I threw myself at the feet of the Blessed Mother. To my surprise, as I prayed about the future, she revealed something startling about my past. She showed me she had been with me through it all.

I let out a sigh as my mind drifted back. I began to shake my head as the dominos of my life started dropping before my eyes.

I realized that in Saginaw, it was *Mother Mary* who brought me and my sexuality questions to the Franciscan priest. In Boston, it was *she* who walked with me right past the doors of the porn store. *She* invited me to evangelize on the streets with the Society of *Our Mother of Peace*. It was *she* who brought me to Declan, whom she had healed at *Lourdes*. In the prayer group, it was *she* who had me lead the *Rosary*. And each summer, *she* brought me joy at the Novena to *Our Lady of Mount Carmel*.

I drew in a deep breath and slowly exhaled as the thoughts continued to cascade. I remembered on our wedding day how my unbelieving bride placed the rose at the foot of the *statue of Mary*. How Mary was the *Patroness* of the Society of St. Vincent de Paul. How I had consecrated my life to Jesus through *her*. How in Medjugorje I had seen the miracle of the sun on a pilgrimage to *honor her*. And how it was *Mary, Our Lady of Guadalupe* who brought us the $700,000 to help her foster children.

I rested in the hands of my Mother. Then I began to slowly pace around my office. Yes, I'd need a lot of help to establish a new publishing company, but how could I be afraid? Scripture tells us 365 times to *be not afraid*. And the Mother who had helped me *all my life* would be there at my side.

I was filled with joy! *Crazy* joy! There was only one obstacle. Without any money, how could I quit my job and start this apostolate?

HANDS FROM ABOVE

The answer came through my 92-year-old mom, Millie. On my 60th birthday, she called from her home in Texas, and in her sweet, loving, inimitable way, she sang *Happy Birthday* to me, the same way she did every year.

I got even more emotional when she ended the call by saying, "Christopher, I'm ready to go home. There's nothing left for me to do here. I'm asking the Lord to take me."

The very next day, Mom woke up in terrible pain. My brother took her to the hospital, and a large tumor was discovered in her stomach. This was strange, since Mom had never complained of stomach pain.

Two days later, she survived a three-hour operation. I flew in to be with her. The tumor was removed, but almost immediately, other fast-growing tumors appeared, and the surgeon said there was nothing further he could do.

A nurse, my mom's longtime friend, drove from Detroit to Texas to comfort her. Mom's best friend, Kathy Fauser, was constantly by her side. Three days after surgery, Mom asked my brother, Joe, to open up her well-worn phone directory. We sat in amazement as Mom called person after person, and told them she was dying. Then she asked each one how *they* were doing, and doled out sage, and often hilarious, advice. Her lines were so sharp and funny, the nurse started writing them down. We marveled at the 92-year-old dying patient *serving others,* bringing *them* laughter and comfort. The dying woman who was "Irish with a shot of Scotch" was showing us how to mix sorrow with a shot of joy.

On January 23rd, the Lord welcomed my mom home. We buried her next to my dad. The temperature was in the twenties as we laid her to rest, back in Detroit. Huge snowflakes fell all around. Mom would have said, *"Isn't this beautiful!?"*

With my beloved parents, Ed and Millie

In the spring, my youngest brother and I settled my mom's estate. I was determined to use my inheritance for good. What greater good could I do than work fulltime for my Heavenly Mother?

I resigned from Angels' Arms, and with my mom as our first donor, I took the hand of Mary. I formed a not-for-profit publishing apostolate. My friend, Deby, inspired me to name the apostolate, Mater Media. As *Mater Dei* is translated *the Mother of God*, *Mater Media* is *the Mother of Media.*

In dying, my mom gave birth to a rock star. Manny Morrison, an aspiring singer/songwriter, is the protagonist in my first novel. In the midst of ambition, lust, murder, an unplanned pregnancy, a near death experience, and fame, Manny and his NFL superstar pal and two young Catholic women face the challenges of modern culture and discover the *theology* of the body.

It's sacred irony that God is using this reformed slave of sexual appetites to impart the Church's teachings on the truth and beauty of human sexuality. My hope is that Manny and friends will inspire meaningful dialogue between many teens and their parents, teachers, and counselors.

A LOVING TOUCH

You may be wondering if I ever found true love. Well, I met this beautiful, charming woman who recognized me from my TV days. Her name was Kathleen. She was joyful in spirit and very attractive, slender with long, beautiful, curly red hair.

We were both working on our first novels. We'd meet at coffee shops and share our writing progress. Before long, I asked Kathleen if she wanted to date. My big concern was age. I was 60 and she was 42. She said age didn't matter.

After doing the dinner-and-a-movie thing for a while, we flew to Chicago to celebrate the completion of my novel's first draft. We went on August 15th, the Feast of the Assumption of the Blessed Mother into Heaven. I thought it was a great day to say, "Thanks, Mom!" We celebrated the Feast at St. Peter's Church in the Loop.

We cruised the Chicago River, checked out the masterpieces at the Art Institute, and strolled the streets of the city before sharing a romantic dinner at Osteria Via Stato. Sharing a mutual appreciation of the principles of the theology of the body, we stayed in separate rooms.

I went to sleep a happy man.

The next morning at breakfast, as raindrops began to fall, I stole my first kiss under the umbrella of a little sidewalk café. We were quickly growing closer than friends and writing companions.

A couple of months later, we visited my beloved Boston. We strolled through the city hand-in-hand. On the brick sidewalk of Tremont Street, we came across a forlorn man sitting against a building. We invited him into a nearby McDonald's and bought him a meal.

I showed Kathleen where O'Reilly and I lived as neighbors when we did Boston TV. We hit one of my favorite areas, the North End, where she delighted in the aromas wafting forth from the Italian restaurants and pastry shops and expresso cafes that lined Hanover Street. Over fine wine, delicious entrees, and sweet gelato, the walls came down.

I opened up about my past heartbreaks and found compassion in the eyes of this devout woman. She readily shared *her* story with a frankness I found refreshing. I longed to share everything with her. I was in love.

Kathleen was loving Boston, and I was loving that she was loving a city that I loved! I confided that I could easily move back to Boston, that it would be a great place to write. I knew she would never leave her mom and St. Louis, but she said that the rental of a Boston brownstone would be a great place to stoke the creative writing fire. I loved that idea!

As the breezy days of late October gave way to the chill of November, I began looking for a house. I was living in a downtown apartment building and wanted to find a peaceful place to write. Kathleen knew that I liked openness and light, and she located a home online that featured a huge *wall of windows.*

We met at the house. It backed to beautiful, hilly woods, but it was in *terrible* shape. It had been on the market for 475 days, and vacant for 300 days, and had gone into foreclosure. It had listed for more than $400,000, slipped into the $300s, and then dipped into the $200s.

Kathleen did not like the home, and not just because it needed work. She said with all the windows, it would be like living in a glass house, with very little privacy. I had a different view. I *loved* the high ceilings and the openness. I didn't plan to waltz naked in front of the wall of windows, so I wasn't worried about privacy.

Anyway, my relationship with Kathleen was *far* more important than *any* house, and there were plenty of houses we could choose from if we got married. The calendar drifted into December and I was deep into the most beautiful relationship of my life.

Kathleen was everything I'd been looking for. Attractive, feminine, smart, loving, caring, spicy, passionate, and deeply devout in her Catholic Faith with a hunger for spiritual growth.

Passionately in love as well, Kathleen came up with an idea that would change our lives. She suggested that we make a Novena, which is, in essence, nine days of intense, special prayers for a particular intention. Our intention was to know God's Will regarding marriage. God's Will and ours sometimes coincide, but not always.

We started the Novena the next day. Kathleen's mom joined us in praying it. You can't have too many prayer partners. We invoked the intercession of St. Philomena, one of Kathleen's favorite saints.

What happened is difficult to describe. The day after the Novena ended, I was *overwhelmed* with the knowledge that God had answered our prayers. It was His Will that Kathleen and I *not* get married.

It's not always easy to discern God's Will, what He wants us to do, what His plans are for us. But in this moment, I knew with *absolute certainty.*

I called Kathleen and told her of the answer I had received, and of its clarity. I told her that God did not reveal to me the reason, or reasons, for His answer, but that He had made it fully and totally clear.

I could tell that Kathleen did not expect this answer. I completely understood. She was longing for the love and intimacy of marriage. I was consumed with an incredible sorrow for her, which went beyond my own personal disappointment. And my disappointment was deep. I thought I had found the wonderful, loving person with whom I could enjoy the fabulous, loving marriage I had envisioned for *decades*. I cannot articulate the shock this was for *both* Kathleen and me.

Yet amazingly, I did not feel despair. I truly did not. I had gotten to the point where I knew that doing God's Will is the most important thing. God's Will was absolutely clear to me. It seemed to *me* that marrying Kathleen would be best, but I trusted that if God was telling us "No," then *most certainly*, it would *not* be best!

I reflected on my earlier mistakes in affairs of the heart. I *certainly* thought that proposing to Sylvia was best, or I never would have done it back in 1996. And *certainly*, I thought marrying Natalie was best, or I wouldn't have walked down the aisle with her in 2002. From this perspective, I knew it was *certainly possible* that I was mistaken again.

And the Lord blessed me with the belief—the deep, total, comforting *belief*—that He was saving me—*and Kathleen*— from what He knew would *not* be best for us.

A SURPRISING TOUCH

I was always looking for the perfect woman. It only took me 40 years to realize—the Perfect Woman was Mary!

Perfect only begins to describe her. Daughter of the Father, Mother of the Son, Spouse of the Holy Spirit, and Mother to me. Perfect indeed!

Through the lust of my college years, the unending search, all the blind dates, the roller coaster relationships, the broken engagement, the annulled marriage, the last beautiful romance: Mary was always there.

As a good mother always wants to find the perfect spouse for her children, my Mother was leading me to the intimacy I always hungered for. Mary brought me to her Son and my Brother who said, "Have I got the bride for you!"

The passion I was seeking to give to *one woman* was a passion He wanted me to unleash upon *the whole world.*

My bride was working in a wheelchair as a greeter at Walmart. My bride was an elderly, semi-bed ridden woman in the inner city. My bride was a guy in a workshop stuffing envelopes with a smile on his face. My bride was a black kid who broke the color barrier at my high school. My bride was a red-haired lion tamer with her head on my shoulder on a bus. My bride was a friend who sucked me into a California AMWAY meeting. My bride was a hockey star who scored the winning goal against the Russians. My bride took me out to sell replacement windows. My bride was a scar-faced man who threatened my life. My bride was a broadcast executive who fired me. My bride sat next to me on the news set. My bride was totally different than I ever imagined.

HANDING IT OFF

I bought the "glass house." Someone suggested I raze it, but I asked the Holy Family to *raise it up*—to give honor and glory to God. The Lord sent a host of skilled craftsmen to turn a tomb into a home.

Dustin Whitsett's young wife was pregnant with their first child.

Painting was his thing. He assembled a team that ascended the 20-foot and 30-foot and 40-foot heights to scrape, prep, and paint the entire interior and exterior. I prayed for them every day. I didn't want anyone laying down his life.

Every inch of flooring had to be replaced—the dog-urine stained carpeting, the black-and-white, diner-style tile in the kitchen, the wall-to-wall filth in the bathrooms. Jerry the Floor Man and his crew took on the task. They replaced two non-flushing toilets before they laid the bathroom tile. On their knees, they measured and cut and installed a houseful of carpeting in one night.

Outside, rotten deck boards were marked off by the yellow caution tape used at murder scenes. Dustin's uncle, John Perrotti, brought in two woodworkers who removed, cut, and replaced 42 long boards, turning a death trap into a restored, 62-foot deck surrounded by woods.

John tore out and rebuilt the kitchen, which came with no working appliances. I bought a refrigerator, stove, microwave, dishwasher, and garbage disposal. The day after I moved in, the old air conditioner stopped working. No surprise!

The roots of a spectacular weeping cherry tree had pushed up portions of the front sidewalk. Some terrific cement guys re-routed and laid a walkway that would welcome guests, not injure them.

The mother-in-law suite was converted into a headquarters for the Mother of Media—75 feet of wall space covered with huge white boards, modern technology, and a large Divine Mercy image of Jesus.

After 14 weeks of work, the last of the mighty workmen were about to depart, but I had a request.

"Hey, guys! Can you hang a picture for me?"

I knew they were tired. "Yeah, sure, Zip. How big is it?"

I brought out the 3 x 4 portrait of Our Lady of Guadalupe. They sighed, but within minutes, they had it in a most prominent place, visible to all.

"Great job, guys!"

"You're welcome, Zip. Anything else?"

I looked at these men who had poured themselves out for so long to make this once-beaten structure into something special. "Well, would you like to hang another one?"

"A little smaller?"

"No. A little bigger."

I brought out a life-size image of the Risen Jesus on canvas.

"Where does it go?"

I gulped. "Up there." I pointed to a spot about 25 feet up on the atrium wall.

What transpired was harrowing. John placed his ladder on the lower level and ascended, step by careful step. His sidekick, Brent, held the painting over the railing on the upper level, and extended it toward John. For a moment, I thought John was going down. Somehow, he kept his balance, grabbed the painting, and got the wire hung on the hooks.

John descended, and walked up the stairs. He gave me a rueful look. "Now—*that's* it, right?"

"John, I've got an *even bigger one* for the living room near the ceiling..." I paused for effect, "...but it hasn't been delivered yet."

"So sorry we'll have to miss it!"

Two weeks later, my neighbor, Deacon Dan Raidt, came over to hang the 5 x 7 foot reproduction of Da Vinci's *Last Supper*. Another high wire act.

To a kitchen wall, we applied the words of Mary:

"My soul proclaims the greatness of the Lord; my spirit rejoices in God my Savior."

I asked some young people to place holy words high up on my dining room wall, but the forces of evil interfered. We tried Super Glue, Gorilla Glue, Gorilla Tape, even metal lettering and nails, but the letters kept falling off the wall.

A friend tried to stencil the words on. He fell from his ladder and bruised his tailbone. Unrelenting, I hired two professional wall decorators. While I prayed, they succeeded in permanently applying the words of 1 Thessalonians 5:16-18:

> *"Rejoice always,*
> *never cease praying,*
> *render constant thanks,*
> *for this is God's Will for you in Christ Jesus."*

All in all, more than a dozen craftsmen renovated the "glass house" into a home that feels like a retreat center. And they fashioned the lower level into much more than a man cave—the headquarters of Mary's ministry: Mater Media.

THE LORD'S HANDIWORK

I now see *my soul* as a far greater renovation project than my house. Jesus began with my interior, once I agreed to the work. He stooped down and—bit by bit—removed what was rotten and stained in me.

Consecrating my life to Jesus through Mary ripped out and replaced my internal plumbing. The Sacrament of Reconciliation effectively flushes my system, keeping me connected to the fountain of the Lord's ocean of love and mercy.

I built my life around appetites that drove me to self-satisfaction, but that structure's been replaced by my original design. God made me for more than me. Less for me *is* more.

My storytelling, humor, and romantic idealism are meant to be a fountain of grace and mercy for others. We all need to be reminded that deep down, we yearn for far more than money, achievement, success, sexual gratification, or a world title for our favorite sports team. We thirst for God's love.

The irony is that Jesus, my master plumber, is thirsty Himself. He has worked so long and so hard for us! He thirsts to love us, and to be loved by us!

The Lord is continuing to rebuild my life through Mary. I try to let the love of her Son shine through me to every "bride" I meet. To be candid, sometimes the work seems like a *scraping and painting project that never ends*, but with each brush stroke, little by little, brighter colors are revealed. The work goes on, but I've learned to trust the General Contractor.

You see, my story is a kaleidoscope of other people's stories. God has shown me that each encounter we share creates a breathtaking and beautiful mosaic. I have a rich and meaingful story to tell because of the eternal value of all the *other people* in it. Each face, each touch, each smile, each tear, each moment...matters.

And it's not just my life that is meant *for a greater purpose.* Your life is no less precious to God. Your story is no less important. Your internal renovation can be just as spectacular in His capable and loving hands.

I just pray that your soul requires less demolition than mine!

Renovated entry to the home of Mater Media

GRATIAS

I'm extremely grateful to all who helped to make this book a reality. Special thanks:

To the Father and the Son and the Holy Spirit, the Trinity from Whom all blessings flow.

To Mary, the Mother of God, my Mother, the Mother of Media, for calling me to serve in your apostolate, for the grace to do it, and for being with my every step of the way.

To my special intercessors St. Joseph, St. Paul, St. Francis de Sales, St. Francis of Assisi, St. Vincent de Paul, Blessed Frederic Ozanam, Blessed Rosalie Rendu, St. Louise de Marillac, St. Elizabeth Ann Seton, and all the Vincentian saints in Heaven, and all the Vincentian souls in Purgatory.

To my beloved deceased for your daily intercession: Mom, Dad, Declan, Anne, and Sandy.

To Cathy Gilmore, for your brilliant direction in editing, for defining the essence of the story, for helping me to recognize and describe my "brides." Gotta *hand* it to you for the titles.

To Trese Gloriod, for a terrific layout and design from cover to cover.

To Molly Moran, for all you have done for the apostolate, for your brilliance in sharpening the focus, and for your love and joy in service.

To Eric Gaulden, for your gifts in moving the project forward in the beginning.

To Maggie Singleton, for your keen eye.

To my super friend, Bill O'Reilly, for encouraging me—and for putting up with me—for more than 40 years.

MATER
MEDIA

Mater is the Latin word for Mother. As *Mater Dei* is translated
The *Mother of God*, *Mater Media* means *The Mother of Media*.
This apostolate is consecrated to Our Blessed Mother.

The VISION of Mater Media

To feed those who are hungry to know the truth.

To satisfy the thirst of souls who are parched with doubt.

To clothe souls that sin has stripped of their dignity.

To invite homeless souls into the shelter of the Church with mercy.

To comfort afflicted souls who need healing in body, mind or spirit.

To remind all of us, as ransomed captives, to bear wrongs patiently, like Jesus.

To honor each person's life, including those who have died, with our prayers.

The MISSION of Mater Media

To write, print, publish, and distribute books that evangelize the Catholic Faith

Mater Media is a not-for-profit apostolate which relies on donations
to continue and further its mission.

You can help Mater Media reach more souls for Christ. Visit:

www.matermedia.org

Share
FOR A GREATER PURPOSE
with Friends

Evangelize the Faith
by sharing
Zip Rzeppa's
joy-filled faith
journey with
others

- Unlimited FREE copies
- Bulk orders welcome

ForAGreaterPurpose.org

Coming Soon:
FOR A GREATER PURPOSE
Audio Book

INVITE ZIP RZEPPA
to Your City or Town

Bring Zip to Your Parish or Conference

Zip Rzeppa travels across the USA to share the message
that every life matters.

Filled with energy, humor, and wisdom,
Zip's presentations entertain, inspire, and edify

Zip asks for a free will donation to Mater Media
in lieu of a speaker's fee

Put Some Zip in Your Fundraising

As a dynamic, joy-filled, and humorous speaker/emcee/auctioneer,
Zip Rzeppa has helped to raise millions of dollars for religious and
not-for-profit organizations, among them:

- Society of
  St. Vincent de Paul
- Angels' Arms
- Serra Club
- Family Resource Center,
- Catholic Family Services
- Vitae Foundation

- MERS Goodwill Industries
- Carmelite Sisters of the
  Divine Heart of Jesus
- Daughters of St. Paul
- Little Sisters of the Poor
- Covenant Network
- Teens2Teens

To invite Zip Rzeppa to Speak or Fundraise, visit
www.matermedia.org

Order FREE copies of the
CURRICULUM FOR TEACHERS
AND STUDENTS

Written by Director of Religious Education and Confirmation Teacher Margaret Marino, the Workbook includes a guided 10-week curriculum for young teens and confirmation classes presenting authentic Catholic moral teaching in creative ways

Week 1	Prayer
Week 2	Friendship
Week 3	Making God a Part of Your Life
Week 4	Temptation
Week 5	Finding Christ in All People
Week 6	Charity
Week 7	When You are Down and Out…
Week 8	Consequences
Week 9	Forgiveness
Week 10	The Eucharist

The Workbook is packed with material from Scripture and the Catechism of the Catholic Church. Includes an Examination of Conscience in preparation for Reconciliation, plus projects emphasizing the virtues and the lives of the saints.

HELP US HELP SOULS

Mater Media distributes FREE copies of
For A Greater Purpose to inspire souls at:

Parishes   Hospitals

Conferences   Nursing Homes

Retreats   Assisted Living Centers

Seminars   Retirement Homes

HELP US HELP TEENS

Mater Media distributes FREE copies of
My Rock & Salvation to evangelize teens at:

Schools   Rehabilitation Facilities

Youth Groups   Pregnancy Resource Centers

Teen Retreats   Conferences

HELP US HELP TEACH

Mater Media distributes FREE copies of
Teacher & Student editions of
My Rock & Salvation WORKBOOKS to:

Counselors   Confirmation Teachers

Parents   Youth Ministers

Make your tax-deductible donation at

www.matermedia.org

Mater Media collaborates with those who positively impact the culture through various forms of media, including:

Metanoia Films

Producers of the award-winning and acclaimed movies, *Bella* and *Little Boy*, with plans to produce the prequel to *The Passion of the Christ*.

Novo Media Group

Developing and producing superior films, TV shows and digital media that positively impacts and inspires the audience.

Movies to Movement

Working to change the culture by producing, marketing and distributing films that celebrate life, love and beauty.

Mysterium Records

A record label, production house, and event production company that popularizes and celebrates all things sacred by creating music, books and events for the universal Church.

For information about

Mater Media's collaborations, visit:

www.matermedia.org

MATER
MEDIA

Moments Matter.

Mater Media Prayer

Blessed Virgin Mary,
I cover myself with your protection.
Defend me and all your children,
from everything that would harm
our souls!

Mary, Mother of Media,
please ask your Son, Jesus,
to fill me with the light of His love
to overcome the darkness
in our world.

Amen

MATER
MEDIA

Make A Difference.